The Family Covenant

Love and Forgiveness in the Christian Home

by Dr. Dennis B. Guernsey

David C. Cook Publishing Co.
Elgin, Illinois/Weston, Ontario

David C. Cook Publishing Co.
Elgin, Illinois—Weston, Ontario
THE FAMILY COVENANT
Love and Forgiveness in the Christian Home
© 1984 Dennis B. Guernsey

Published by David C. Cook Publishing Co.
850 N. Grove Ave., Elgin, IL 60120
Edited by Janet L. Kobobel
Cover design by Katherine Roundtree
Printed in the United States of America
Library of Congress Catalog Number 83-51603
ISBN: 0-89191-843-4

To my mother, Merle Guernsey,
and my mother- and father-in-law,
Jean and Elton Lorenz,
who through their love for me
have modeled the meaning of covenant.

TABLE OF CONTENTS

Grace Alone

"It's tough enough living the Christian life,
but living it in my family
is next to impossible."

The words were spoken by an angry and frustrated mother with two teenaged sons and an absent, workaholic husband. She had concluded: It's one thing to be a Christian, it's another to live the Christian life in the context of one's family.

Her complaint was typical. It was hard to live as a Christian when the work of raising her sons had fallen on her shoulders. The weight was proving to be more than she could bear. Her oldest son was in a state of rebellion, and the youngest was performing far below his potential in school. Layered on top of that state of affairs was her growing dissatisfaction with her marriage.

Her response was predictable. She became depressed. In desperation she turned to a counselor. Her previous encounter with her pastor had proved to be less than helpful, not because of his intent but because of his knee-jerk solution.

"The biggest problem you have is your husband," he said. "If he were providing leadership in the home, everything else would fall into place."

While her pastor's response was true in part, she knew that his advice was deficient on the whole. There was something more to the problem, but she didn't know what it was.

She did know that the pain from the immediate problem had become unbearable. She needed help, and the solution to her problems was deeper and more profound than any that had been offered by her mentors.

She was in a state of anomie, defined by sociologists as a state of mind when the rules and norms of the past are not working. The person is faced with dilemmas for which previous solutions are ineffective.

That mother's despair symbolizes the perplexity of those of us who are trying to make Christianity work in our everyday lives. The hardest place of all to apply it seems to be in our families.

2

Three-Tiered Solutions

Those of us who minister in the helping professions, and those of us who can identify with the mother's pain whatever our profession, are faced with finding solutions on three levels.[1] The first two are mentioned here only in passing. The purpose of this book is to deal with the third.

The first level is the psychological. Whether we are professional, pastor, or neighbor, the tendency is to begin here. This is where we have been conditioned by our educational system to begin. We tend to ask: What's going on inside her head that would explain her problem? Is it an issue of her low self-esteem? Or is it a matter of unresolved "object" conflicts?[2] Whatever, the psychological issues have been thoroughly explored in contemporary literature and need not be covered here.

The second level deals with structure and system.[3] We ask: What are the relationships that are dysfunctional, or not functioning normally? What needs to happen for those relationships to function well again?

This is the level that most of us, both lay and professional, would turn to as our second choice. On the face of it, for those of us who deal with families, it would seem to be the most natural place to begin. What are the family's communication patterns?[4] What, if any, are the "double binds" or conflicting communications?[5] Again, contemporary literature is rife with solutions.

But there is a third and, in my opinion, a deeper and more subtle level. It is the level of the theological. What are the doctrinal issues that tilt her perceptions and responses to others?

The difficulty with answers at this level is that they are hard to unpack. They often exist deep within us, where we form assumptions about how we live. They operate much like the foundations of a structure. They are essential to support a building, and they define the shape and form of the building. But for the most part they are unseen, forgotten, and difficult to reach.

In terms of the distressed mother at the beginning of the chapter, the temptation is to approach the problem at the level of the psychological and the structural without touching the theological. But, ultimately, this is the level where we must either begin or end. By all means it is a level that cannot be ignored.

The Theological?

What do I mean by the theological? Recently our family was privileged to host Dr. James Torrance and his wife for dinner. Dr. Torrance, one of the world's leading theologians from the University of Aberdeen in Scotland, recounted a story behind the visit of Pope John Paul to Scotland.

A modest controversy surfaced over the issue of how the moderator of the Church of Scotland should greet the Pope when he welcomed him to their land. The issue involved whether or not he should mention John Knox, the great Reformation hero of Scotland. The irony of the event was that the Pope was to be greeted on the grassy slopes of the kirk, or church, where Knox preached and from whose pulpit the Reformation was launched in Scotland.

The decision was made that the moderator should say, basically, "welcome," and that no mention would be made of Knox.

Torrance's response was filled with passion. "What an opportunity was lost! Rather than just say 'welcome,' if I were the one to greet the Pope, I would have said, 'Dear Brother, we stand in the shadow of the man John Knox who founded the Church of Scotland. The same John Knox who proclaimed *sola gratia,* by grace alone. Because of that grace I extend my hand to you and welcome you to our land.' "

Because of the working of God's grace in his life, Torrance could welcome someone with whom he had distinct differences. But that person was to be treated on gracious terms.

Following Dr. Torrance's visit I was reminded of the principle of *sola gratia.* I was driving home, thinking about the implications of the doctrine of grace in my own life. In particular I had suffered through a difficult time with my

4

family. The specifics escape me now (conveniently), but the reality is still very much with me.

God has dealt with me graciously in Christ, and yet I was dealing with those around me, not according to grace, but according to works. I was intuitively demanding that they perform in order to meet my expectations.

Sola gratia, sola gratia, sola gratia.

The words echoed in my ears. I couldn't hide. My inconsistency was ever before me. Sometimes the way we live and the way we believe are so distant from one another. How can I hold any standard for others but the one God Himself holds for me?

I decided then and there to explore the implications of the doctrine of grace as they related to my life. I was attempting to probe myself at that deep, theological level.

Not at the psychological level. (What's going on in my head?) Not at the structure-and-sytem level. (How can I change the way my relationships function?) But the theological level. I am saved "by grace alone." (What spiritual beliefs am I living out?)

What does it mean to live "by grace alone"?

The answer to that question is at the heart of what this book is about. Simply stated, as children of grace we are to live with one another according to that grace.

But what does that mean? I think it means at least three things.

"Grace alone" involves an unconditional love

I have the privilege of teaching graduate theological students preparing for ministry. One of the courses I team teach is a course on the "Theology of the Family." Part of what we ask our students to do in the course is to interact with basic words that have theological connotations. We ask them to respond to those words and concepts from the perspective of their own families of origin, that is, the families they grew up in.

One of the words we ask them to interact with is the word "covenant." At the heart of this word is the idea of unconditional love.

It's fascinating to read the essays that are returned to us. Many, if not a majority, report that they struggle with the word and wonder if they have ever loved someone else or have been loved by someone else unconditionally, just to love or be loved as if there were no end.

What does it mean to love unconditionally?

Willing to Accept Less than Perfect

In the first place, an unconditional love is *a love that is willing to accept less than that which is perfect, even sometimes less than the best.*

Behind this idea is the problem of shame. Unconditional love doesn't try to control others by means of manipulating their natural tendency to experience shame when they fail.

Let me illustrate what I mean. Our oldest daughter, Sheryl, possesses the uncanny ability to puncture my parental balloon. One day we were sitting around the kitchen table, and she said, "You know, Dad, living with you is like competing in a high jump. Sometimes I get out there and you say, 'Sheryl, here's the standard. Go for it.' Then I run out into whatever I'm doing, and I stand at the side of the high jumping pit. Then I approach the bar and leap over it, and more often than not, I clear it. When I do, you're one of the most enthusiastic and excited cheerleaders in the world.

"You did it! You made it! That's great!" you exclaim.

"Then, Dad, you say, 'Now we're going to move the standard up one more inch.'"

Thoughtfully she looked me in the eye and said, "It's as if life with you is always one inch higher than I can reach."

Needless to say, her cheerful but pointed confrontation forced me to look at myself and my relationship with her.

Psychologically, I understood what was happening. A significant other in Sheryl's life was moving the bar of his approval up to the place where, inevitably, she would fail. The end result of that demand is the feeling of shame. It's the feeling that you're always letting somebody down. That you're never good enough. And shame is the opposite of unconditional love.

My sense tells me that unconditional love recognizes that it is our nature as humans to "knock the bar off." God does not demand perfection from me; He demands submission and faithfulness. Sometimes we mix the issues and get confused.

As Christians it's easy to be responsive to the teachings of Paul about how we are to "press toward the mark for the prize of the high calling of God in Christ Jesus." But then we lose the flexibility to accept not being able to always meet the standard. There is a natural tension at the point of failure that we need to learn to accept. The issues just don't fall into neat and tidy piles.

Grace alone involves a love that accepts less than the best sometimes.

Doesn't Take Everything Personally

There is another dynamic that often takes place in families that is the obverse, or counterpart, of unconditional love. It has to do with guilt. Said in another way, *unconditional love doesn't turn each and every issue into an issue involving personal acceptance or rejection.*

Some of you, I'm sure, have seen the telephone commercial on television in which you, the viewer, are being encouraged to call long distance. A young man is animatedly dialing the phone. The screen splits, and you listen in on his conversation with his mother.

"Hi, Mom," he says.

At the other end, his mother answers, "How come you never call your mother?"

His frustrated response is classic: "Mom, I'm calling you now." What you don't hear are the epithets muttered under his breath.

The emotional tone of the ad is to point out the guilt between them. By implication, viewers are asked if they feel guilty for not calling someone.

How true to life. The mother felt rejected when her son didn't call. "How come you always let me down? Why are you *doing this to me?*" her tone demanded.

Have you ever had the feeling that when you have done something—or haven't done something—you have hurt a significant someone, and that person feels rejected? He or she has made the issue one of personal acceptance or rejection.

Many of us walk around with a pervasive feeling of guilt. It's not shame that we feel. It's the feeling that somehow we have hurt or are likely to hurt another who is important to us. We feel that we'll never please the one in question.

Everything becomes a personal issue. If the room isn't clean, if the dishes are left dirty on the counter, somehow we *meant* to hurt them. The issue that forms the axis around which everything turns is guilt. We intended to reject the person by our actions.

Whatever unconditional love is, it isn't a relationship predicated on the axis of guilt. Performance is an issue, but it isn't a personal issue. (We'll discuss performance and permissiveness in the next chapter.)

Doesn't Give Up and Quit

There is a third dimension to unconditional love. *It is the kind of love that holds on after human instincts demand you give up on the other person.*

I am reminded of the story recorded in Paul's first letter to the Corinthians. In Corinth there was a man who was living with his mother-in-law in open sin, and the sin was a disgrace to the testimony of the church. Paul's instruction was for the church to cast the man from its fellowship, a very harsh action. Paul could be a hard taskmaster.

However, we are later told in II Corinthians that Paul instructed the church at Corinth to restore a man because he had suffered enough. Some scholars believe the man in I Corinthians and the man in II Corinthians are the same. If so, the story is descriptive of the tension between unconditional love and discipline. On the one hand, Paul instructs the church to discipline the man and to do so harshly. On the other hand, when the discipline seems to have worked, Paul doesn't give up. He says to restore the man to fellowship.

In terms of grace alone and unconditional love, God never gives up. The Scripture is full of accounts in which God disciplines but never gives up. His relationship with humanity is replete with illustrations of His patience and longsuffering. God always provides a place to come home to when we have wandered far off. God's love never gives up.

The theological issue for you and for me is: Are we quick to give up on others or are we quick to believe that others have given up on us? Do relationships seem to hang together by the thin thread of our performance?

When we live in the shadow of shame or guilt, the natural assumption is that, in the face of our failure, others have given up or are about to give up on us.

Because of grace alone that is never the case with God. His love is unending and steadfast, based upon the constancy of His character and not upon our performance.

When Paul writes, "Love never fails," he is saying that love's unconditional character provides us with the ability to keep going on, that this kind of love perseveres.

Unconditional love, therefore:

1. Is willing to accept less than perfect.
2. Doesn't take everything personally.
3. Doesn't give up.

Grace alone, however, implies more.

"Grace alone" involves uncondi- tional acceptance

Unconditional acceptance is at the heart of what James Torrance was saying. Pope John Paul was someone with whom the Church of Scotland had dramatic differences. And yet, by grace alone, Torrance could say, "I accept you even though I do not agree with you. Because God has accepted me in Christ, I am open to accepting you for who you are."

What is it that is implied in this kind of acceptance? Again, let me suggest three dimensions:

Distinguishes Between Unity and Uniformity

In the first place, *unconditional acceptance distinguishes between unity and uniformity.*

It's easy to accept you if you are exactly like I am. Uniformity demands that we must all be the same, that we all look alike, that we all talk alike, that we all dress alike.

We often see uniformity in action in our churches. Someone walks in, and we can tell immediately that the person doesn't fit. His hair is too long, or her dress is too unusual, or his skin is the wrong color, or some other characteristic is deemed wrong because it's different from ours. The natural instinct is to create distance between us and the ones who are different. In the creation of that distance, they come to feel unwanted, and naturally so.

Unconditional acceptance, I am suggesting, is the openness that says, "What is important is that we be one, not that we be the same." The genius of the church ought to be this openness to one another. And if this is true in the church, why not at home?

In terms of the family, the tendency is to place greater importance on issues of conformity rather than upon the nature of the relationship between us. In family therapy we call this the difference between communication and metacommunication.[6]

Most of us focus on content or communication issues when we deal with one another, especially when it comes to conflict between us.

For example, suppose my wife and I are having an argument over money. The tendency will be to try to outthink, outtalk, and outwit one another. (I've even been known to try intimidation when it appeared that I was losing an argument.)

However, more important are the meta issues: *How* we talk to one another about what we talk about. Do we listen to one another, or do we interrupt? Do we use sarcasm and cynicism, or do we say what we mean? Irrespective of how angry we get with one another, do we respect the other person's right to have an opinion different from our own?

Boiled down to its basics, "how" is more important than "what" in effective communication. And it's this dimension of acceptance that ultimately allows us to live together as Christians.

Values Diversity

A second facet of this kind of acceptance is, in many ways, the flip side of the first. *Not only does unconditional acceptance distinguish between unity and uniformity, but it, therefore, also values diversity.*

Grace allows people to be dissimilar and even glories in that diversity.

When it comes to your family, have you noticed that the son or daughter you are most likely to have difficulty with is the one who sticks out and is the odd ball? Parents often thank God for the children who fit in and who are compliant. They're on time. They sit or stand still. In some ways you can forget about them because they seem to raise themselves.

Then there are the kids who are diverse, even sometimes perverse. They're the ones who are climbing the trees higher than is safe. When they don't come home at night, you say to yourself, "Well, they'll come home when they're hungry." They seem to be straining at the limits of the rules, and often you are at the end of your patience. After a point there's something inside you that wearies of their diversity. The bottom line is that they don't want to do things your way, and they seem to have been that way all of their lives.

The tendency is to want to take that creativity, that freedom of spirit, grab it, shake it, and put a lid on it. What we want is to press that diversity through a kind of extrusion process (shaping by force) that yields as an end product replicas of ourselves.

But wouldn't it be frightening if all there were in the world were "little you's " and "little me's"?

God, on the other hand, has a marvelous sense of diversity. He values in the church the meta issue of acceptance and calls us to glory in the fact that we are different. We are one, though many. There is a place for us all. The church is not meant to be a cookie-cutter kind of place where we all act, look, and smell alike.

So it can be in families. Diversity can be valued.

Inclusive and Not Exclusive

Third, *unconditional acceptance is inclusive and not exclusive.*

One of the most significant needs for all humans is the need to belong. In fact, much of human behavior can be interpreted as attempting to meet this need. In terms of the doctrine of "grace alone," God has made us all acceptable in Christ. Through His Son, God has made provision for everyone who comes to Him to relate to Him.

But exposure to God's love and acceptance is often not enough. More often than not it needs to be wrapped up in the acceptance by others for it to be personally experienced.

I remember how God's love first became real to me. I was an eighteen-year-old straight off the streets of the harbor area of Los Angeles. My hair was cut in a flattop, and my walk was the swagger of a street kid. Deep inside I knew I wasn't tough, but on the outside I tried to carry it off.

My best friend was dating a girl from the other side of town. Our strategy was for me to go with him to her house and for me to occupy the mother while he "occupied" the daughter. That's when I learned to drink coffee—as a way of diverting the mother's attention. We would arrive at their doorstep and inevitably would be invited in.

"How about a cup of coffee?" would be the first words. I'd accept, and the mother and I would drink coffee and talk about anything and everything. There seemed to be, figuratively, a sign that said "Welcome."

Soon, I came to realize that the family was Christian, and part of its commitment to Christ involved being hospitable.

After a while I told my friend that what we were doing just wasn't right. He agreed, and we stopped our duplicity.

Soon afterwards we were invited to go with them to church. Even though I had rarely attended a church, I was open to going with them because they had opened their door and had welcomed me in. Within a month I had heard the gospel and had received the gift of God's love in Christ.

It's been more than 25 years since then. I'm now a father with two attractive daughters.

One day my daughter brought this young man home to meet me. He wanted to date my daughter. He wasn't a Christian. Everything about him reeked of his pagan ways. I retreated to our kitchen, and God seemed to remind me of another day and time. Another kitchen table where a gracious Christian lady said, "Welcome. Would you like a cup of coffee?" Those folks had accepted me when I didn't fit, when I didn't belong, and when there was nothing winsome about me. Because of their love and acceptance, I came to know and understand the love of God.

With some difficulty, I turned on my heels, walked back into the living room, and said as best as I could, "Welcome. Would you like something to drink?" (Teenagers don't seem to drink coffee these days.)

The memories of that other Christian home still stand out as an example of God's unconditional acceptance. The agency of His love was a Christian home and family. Because they were inclusive, because they included me, I was able to hear the voice of God as one who was inclusive as well. Had they been exclusive or derisive, I imagine the opposite would have been true. I would have reacted negatively and would have rejected their God because I felt I was being rejected.

In a similar way, young people and old are turned off toward God by the exclusivity of His people, people who have forgotten that they know God by grace alone. As hard as it is sometimes for us, we must work toward an inclusive spirit that says, "Welcome to our home. Christ is honored here."

"Grace alone" involves unconditional mercy and forgiveness

Mercy Not Judgment

Words like mercy and forgiveness easily become mere cognitive categories, or categorized pieces of knowledge, unless they are tied to the realities of our lives.

When I think of the word "mercy," I think of a story a friend tells regarding her son. She bought him a skateboard for Christmas. Wrapped in the package were knee pads, a helmet, and instructions on how to ride a skateboard safely. Immediately after he unwrapped his gift, the boy raced outside to try out his new vehicle, accompanied by his mother's stern warning to be careful.

Within a few minutes the mother heard the most awful bellowing outside her front door. Her son stood there, board in hand. He was bleeding from knee and elbow, crying huge, pitiable tears.

He had raced outside and had promptly forgotten every word of caution that she had given. In his childish exuberance, he had careened down a nearby hill and had "wiped out" on a curve, running into the back of a parked car.

That mother's natural instincts were to take her son into the bathroom, boost him onto the bathroom counter and treat his wounds with the most stinging iodine she could find. He had violated her edict and deserved to suffer. Whatever she meted out would have been deserved.

Instead, when faced with his tears, she decided that he had suffered enough. In fact, what was needed was a compassionate rather than a judgmental response. At the heart of her response was the decision to be merciful and not judgmental.

How do we know what it means to be merciful? Because God, in Christ, has acted mercifully toward us. Every one of us deserves to have the most stinging and stringent solution applied to us because of our sin. When God says, "There is none righteous," He is speaking of folk like you and me.

In the practical, day-to-day lives of ordinary people there are countless decisions to be made whether to respond to another mercifully or judgmentally. More often than not, we choose to judge because our authority or advice has been spurned.

However, the longer I have been around families and have been involved in the daily drama of my own, I have concluded that mercy is a desperately needed commodity; judgment is in abundant supply. Grace alone provides us with the option to act mercifully because God daily deals with us so.

Forgiveness Not Punishment

To have been forgiven much is to be expected to forgive.

Several years ago, our oldest daughter was learning to drive. New license in hand, she prevailed on me to let her drive our new VW Rabbit. The rest of us were on our way to church in our other car when I remembered something I wanted her to do. I left the others at church and returned home, pulling our second car up to the curb with its front end sticking into our driveway just a bit.

Sheryl was in the Rabbit, eagerly ready to back out. I gave her the information. She acknowledged it and promptly backed out the car. I sat in the other car and watched her coming. There was nothing I could do. The left rear fender of our new car was creased by the front bumper of our old one.

Sheryl bounded out of the car and I, with rage in my gut, bounded out of mine. Immediately I caught myself. In a split second I remembered when I first learned to drive. On three occasions, involving hundreds of dollars, my own mother had been faced with similar dilemmas. To her credit she responded to each with a statement that still hangs in my mind: "Well, Denny, those things happen."

Her instincts were to forgive and not to punish. My three accidents did not involve deliberate or willful disobedience. They did involve youthful intemperance. Still, her response was, "Those things happen."

I looked at my new car with its first dent, and I heard myself say, "Well, Sheryl, those things happen."

Looking back on that event, I'm not impressed with my response. But I am impressed with the influence the grace of God has over time. The more I am aware of God's forgiveness in my life, the more I am likely to forgive others. I just cannot demand punishment for others when I've been dealt with with forgiveness.

Grace alone implies that God in Christ has loved us with a love that knows no end. Grace alone informs us that Christ has accepted us with all of our faults and all of our shortcomings.

16

God says, "Those things happen." He adds, "Go and sin no more."

Judgment and punishment face toward the past. Mercy and forgiveness face toward the future. It is a future with the cross etched into it as a reminder that we are to live with one another in mercy and forgiveness. We are to bear in mind God's merciful and forgiving act toward us in Christ. Because of the Cross we can face the future and not be captured by the past, neither the past with our own sins, nor the past with the disappointments and hurts inflicted by others.

For us as Christians there is always hope based on the finished work of Christ and oriented to that time when all things will be made new. Because of that hope and in light of that orientation we should be "forgiving one another, as God in Christ forgave you."

Free But Not Cheap

What about the distressed mother who began our chapter, pained by her relationships with her workaholic husband, her rebellious son, and her underachieving son? What would be her response to all of this? If I were she, I would respond, first, with despair. "Unconditional this" and "unconditional that" simply add to the guilt she already feels. Who needs it?

Second, I would respond on the theological level. Sometimes it's hard to be faced with truth about ourselves that doesn't fit our personal view.

In her case, although she identified her mother as one who motivated her children by guilt, it wasn't as easy to evaluate herself. Slowly and inexorably she faced the issues. Her eventual evaluation of her relational and parental style was that she had learned to deal with others in much the same way she herself had been dealt with as a child. The pattern had been set. Now her work as one who loved her family and as one who was committed to live as a Christian was to unlearn much. She decided it would be a hard task, but it would be worth it.

17

It's been several years since she and I first talked, and the reports are good. "I'm not perfect," she says, but she is learning to forgive herself so that she can learn to forgive those closest to her.

She and I both know that this kind of change, like salvation, is free but not cheap. That God is in the business of teaching us to "work out your own salvation with fear and trembling." It's hard work, but it's worth it.

A Brief Summary

*"Grace alone" involves an unconditional love.
   This unconditional love:
      —is willing to accept less than perfect.
      —doesn't take everything personally.
      —doesn't give up and quit.
*"Grace alone" involves unconditional acceptance.
   This unconditional acceptance:
      —distinguishes between unity and uniformity.
      —values diversity.
      —is inclusive and not exclusive.
*"Grace alone" involves unconditional mercy and forgiveness.
   This unconditional mercy and forgiveness:
      —responds with mercy, not judgment.
      —forgives and does not punish.

Covenants
Not
Contracts

Some folks struggle with two seemingly
incongruous facts: We must come to God
by grace and through faith;
we must produce "good works."

We are all aware that we are totally dependent upon God
for eternal life. What, then, is the relationship between this
life of faith and the good works that are to proceed from that
life?

James wrote in his New Testament letter that genuine
faith yields genuine works. The two are inseparable. Even
though you can say one thing and do another, the goal of the
Christian life is to live congruently, or consistently. The
Christian life at this point involves an inevitable tension
between faith and works.

The same tension occurs in families. It comes about in the
relationship between unconditional love and acceptance and
the natural needs for family members to perform their tasks
within the family. How do you unconditionally love and
accept a family member who habitually shirks responsibili-
ties in the home? Is there ever a time when enough is
enough?

Such was the confusion beneath the tension and struggle of
the frustrated mother chronicled in chapter one. She fully
intended to love her family, but it seemed that when she did,
they abused that love and took advantage of her. Her response was to vacillate between the roles of martyr and
dictator. She hated herself for it, but for the life of her, she
couldn't break free of the dilemma. What's a mother to do?

In her case, the dilemma began to be alleviated as she and
I explored the issue at the theological level. In fact, our
interaction proved to be truly liberating for her and might be
for others who can identify with her struggle.

In theological literature the tension she experienced is
expressed in two words: covenant and contract. In the balance of this chapter I will explore the nature and meaning of
those two words, make some applications to family life, and
then end with a look at the tension that typically results from
the interaction between the two.

The nature of "covenant": unconditional commitment

For purposes of our discussion I have taken the word "covenant" to mean a promise or commitment binding two parties to one another unconditionally.[1] The concept is illustrated marvelously by the relationship between God and the nation of Israel as recorded in Deuteronomy 7: 6-9:

> For you [Moses says to the nation] are a people holy to the Lord your God; the Lord your God has chosen you to be a people for his own possession, out of all the peoples that are on the face of the earth. It was not because you were more in number than any other people that the Lord set his love upon you and chose you, for you were the fewest of all peoples; but it is because the Lord loves you, and is keeping the oath which he swore to your fathers, that the Lord has brought you out with a mighty hand, and redeemed you from the house of bondage, from the hand of Pharaoh king of Egypt. *Know therefore that the LORD your God is God, the faithful God who keeps covenant and steadfast love with those who love him and keep his commandments, to a thousand generations,* (RSV, emphasis mine).

We're all aware that according to the Old Testament, Israel wandered all over the map not only literally but also morally and theologically. But God never once annulled the covenant because of their disobedience. True, He became discouraged and disheartened, even to the point of wanting to get out of the whole relationship (cf. Ex. 32: 1-32). But He didn't because Moses reminded Him of His covenant promises.

In the face of disappointment and habitual disillusionment, it is natural and understandable that we become disheartened. Even the best of us do. It's natural to have thoughts and fantasies of wanting out of the covenant, to be free of our promise.

What is of greater importance is not the temptation to leave but the decision to hang in there. Moses prevailed upon God to hold on and to ride it out. God hung on after He wanted to quit *for the sake of the covenant, because He had made a promise.*

Those of us who are married have made a similar promise. We made it when we said our wedding vows: "I take you (my spouse) to be my wedded husband or wife, to love and to cherish, etc., etc., . . . until we are separated by death." Theologically, beneath the wedding ceremony is the principle of covenant. We promise to relate to one another just as God promised to relate to Israel.

In the Face of Failure

But what do you do when your spouse fails you like Israel failed God? The answer to this question forms, in my opinion, a radical Christian approach to marriage. *Implicit in every covenant is the certainty of betrayal. Embedded in every act of covenant-promise is the reality of disillusionment, disobedience, and disheartenment.*[2]

Such is the great example of Hosea in the Old Testament. Remember the story of Hosea. God chose Hosea and his wife Gomer to serve as a metaphor of the relationship between God and Israel.

God instructs Hosea to take Gomer, "a wife of harlotry . . . for the land commits great harlotry by forsaking the Lord" (Hosea 1: 2, RSV). God tells Hosea that He wanted Hosea's relationship with Gomer to reflect what it means to be a covenant people. Gomer was a harlot and would be a harlot. We are told in chapter three of Gomer's continued betrayal: "And the Lord said to me, 'Go again, love a woman who is beloved of a paramour and is an adulteress; even as the Lord loves the people of Israel, though they turn to other gods and love cakes of raisins' " (v. 1, RSV).

I Take You . . .

God's experience with Israel is the archetype, or the model, of a covenant. Consequently, when you commit yourself to another person in marriage, in some ways the wedding vows would be stated better and more realistically if they said, "I take you to be my lawfully wedded spouse with the full knowledge that you are weak as I am weak; that you will be unfaithful as I will be, if not in actuality, then in fantasy; that there will be times when you will disappoint me gravely as I will disappoint you. But in spite of all of this, I commit myself to love you, knowing your weaknesses and knowing the certainty of betrayal."

The approach I am suggesting flows out of normal developmental stages of a marriage. Not every marriage relationship goes through them all, but enough do to make their mention useful.

The first is *the romantic stage.* In this stage each partner says to the other, "I commit myself to you. You are perfect. You're just what I've been looking for. You have no *real* faults. You are ideal." Humbly, the spouse answers, "Yes, I know. I feel the same about you."

Then comes *the bargaining stage.* One morning you wake up and say, "Boy, you're sure not perfect. I tell you what, I'll change if you will." The marital tug-of-war begins.

When that doesn't work, then comes *the coercive stage.* "Boy oh boy, do you have your faults! Whether you like it or not, I'm going to change you. And if I can't, then I'm going to get God to change you."

The person's prayers fill with petitions to God that He

might do a number on the spouse: "Please, Lord, do something about that slob (or that witch) I'm living with." The coercive stage comes when you decide the faults are immovable so you invoke the power of Heaven to bring the weight of God's conviction upon the errant spouse.

After the coercive stage comes *the desperation stage.* "You are nothing but one huge bundle of faults! I'm convinced that not even God can change you; you are the rock even He cannot lift. I want out. I'm gone. Maybe for real. Maybe in my mind. But I am gone."

Last of all, if they can hang in there long enough, comes *the acceptance stage.* "Well, you know what? We both have our faults. As God gives me strength I'll accept your weaknesses, and I hope that you will do the same for me. Frankly, neither of us got much of a winner when we married the other."

The paradox is that when a couple survives to the acceptance stage, often much of the romanticism returns but without the idealism. If such a thing exists, it is romantic realism. It has to do with loving a real and not a made-up person, surviving the storms as well as the becalmed seas.

In the evolution of marriage, as it moves from the romantic stage to the acceptance stage, what gets you through is the covenant. You can endure the times when the tides are out when you believe that the tides will come in again.

The covenant God made with Israel allowed Him to relate to them during the ebb tides. He knew that following their disobedience and His disheartenment would come renewal. Israel would return, and (viewed from a human standpoint) the knowledge of that was enough to provide Him with the motivation to hold on.

So it is with marriage. Sometimes the only motivation that helps us to hold on is the knowledge that a covenant has been made and God's promise that He will keep His promises.

A Future Hope

Covenant, however, doesn't end with a focus on the past and its struggles and disappointments. Covenant doesn't stay in the despairing stage of a relationship. Covenant, because it is based on the faithfulness of God as well as the faithfulness of the covenanting partners, can hope.

In the same way that God knew Israel would come back, I believe God can make our relationships right when they are desperately wrong. Covenant means not only that I am committed to you and you to me, but also that when things go bad I can believe God will breathe new life into a relationship that seems dead.

Hope was what buoyed God in His relationship with Israel (cf. Hosea 2: 16ff). As such, covenant is not that which assigns us to our past but that which orients us to our future.

Sometimes the marriages that are the worst off surprisingly have the greatest hope—if their participants will work at it. The work requires dismantling the marriage and its dysfunction down to the very foundations of the commitment and saying, "We are married. We are committed. As God gives us strength, we will build again."

If there is no commitment, no covenant, there is no will to go on. If there is covenant, you can forgive seventy times seven. You can endure when everything inside you says quit.

Covenant does not consign us to the past and its defeats. Covenant orients us to the hope that our covenant-making God can make all things new in Christ.

The nature of "contract": something for something

25

In contrast to the principle of covenant is the idea of contract. A contract is defined as a legal relationship in which two people or parties bind themselves together based upon mutual conditions and/or performance.[3]

There are healthy contracts. A contract says that if you will do thus-and-so, then I will do thus-and-so.

An example would be a contract I worked out with our daughter Shannon. I said, "Shannon, I will pay for half of your tennis lessons, if you will pay for the other half. If you do not pay for the one half, I will not pay for the other half." Shannon then set about earning the money to pay for her tennis lessons for the summer.

Contracts involve the principle of *quid pro quo*, something for something.

The problem lies not with healthy contracts but with unhealthy ones—contracts that are applied to relationships that are meant to be unconditional and covenantal. Unhealthy—when my love for my spouse or my child is predicated on her performance and not on my commitment. When this happens, resentments build, confusion rules, and the relationship becomes infused with anxiety.

One relationship that is intended to be covenantal is marriage. In particular the sexual union between husband and wife is vulnerable to the abuse of turning the covenant into contract.

I've been a marriage and family therapist for years. I've been around the block many, many times with many, many people. I am convinced that whenever a husband or a wife decides to step outside of the marriage sexually, at the heart of that decision is not lust, but rage and anger.

The scenario goes something like this: "You promised to be sexually responsive to me and I to you. For some reason you have broken your promise to be responsive. Therefore, it gives me the reason (or as some see it, the right) to break my promise to be faithful." The sexual relationship is somehow envisioned as a *quid pro quo*, as something for something. The marriage is experienced as contractual. When this happens, only pain and unhappiness result.

Parenthetically, this is what is partially wrong with many

women's books on marriage written from the perspective that if you want your husband to do something, you should give him what he wants, a sexier partner. The sexual relationship becomes inherently contractual. The sexual relationship is meant to be reciprocal, mutual giving and taking; it is never meant to be contractual (cf. I Cor. 7: 3, 4).

Another relationship that is meant to be covenantal but often becomes contractual is the parent/child relationship.

I remember long ago working with the principal of a Christian day school. He had referred a young child to me because the child was hyperactive in the classroom. The child had been to a specialist, but the pediatrician could not identify any of the neurological patterns that typically accompany hyperkinesis. He felt that the problem might lie in the family and not in the child.

My first interviews with the family seemed to indicate that they were normal, caring people who were befuddled by the behavior of their boy. It was the mother's opinion that the problem was indeed physical and that further tests would prove her right.

The Real Problem

After the third or fourth session, the father asked if he could talk with me alone for just a moment. I agreed, and he sat before me with a pained expression on his face.

"I know what's wrong with my boy," he said.

I nodded and he continued. "It's his relationship with his mother. Oh, I don't want to blame everything on her, but she has this terrible habit. Whenever our son misbehaves and she becomes angry, she stops talking with him. Literally, she just stops any kind of communication. She completely withdraws. It can go on for days until the little guy breaks and comes crawling and sobbing back to her, asking for her forgiveness. Usually by that time he's a basket case, crying and all that. But at least then she does start talking again."

Further involvement with the family and eventually a direct confrontation with the mother proved the father's theory right. The mother was a strict contractualist. She used the withdrawal of love as her means of discipline. Her son was expected to toe the line with her or the relationship was null and void, if only for two or three days. The others in the family had somehow learned to adapt, but the child hadn't and he was paying the price. The schoolroom behavior was the uncontrolled expression of his anxiety, and the anxiety proceeded directly out of the contractual relationship he had with his mother. As far as I know, the mother never faced her contribution to the boy's problems. Contracts had become a way of life.

Said succinctly, *contracts become destructive when they replace covenants in relationships that are meant to be covenantal.*

The dilemma: legalism

The dilemma we face is one of legalism. Most of us have heard or used the term. Usually we think of a list of rules or regulations, the naughty nine, or the terrible ten. However, for purposes of our discussion, legalism will be defined as changing into contracts those relationships that are intended to be covenants. It is a preoccupation with rules to the detriment of relationship.

Let me illustrate the difference between rules within a covenantal relationship and legalism. In God's covenant with us He says, "I have loved you. I have redeemed you. You are My people and I am your God." The statements are all in the indicative case. They all end with a period. "Therefore," He says, "you shall have no other gods before Me. You shall not murder. You shall not commit adultery, etc. . . ."

What God says to us is that because of His unremitting love for us and His unconditional commitment to us, He has the right to have expectations. Demands are made based upon that covenantal relationship. Because of His unconditional love, acceptance, mercy, and forgiveness, He has certain expectations of us and reserves the absolute right to make certain demands on us.[4]

Legalism occurs when the covenant is flipped and in a sense turned inside out. Listen to the subtleties of the contract in contrast to the covenant: "If you keep My commandments, have no other gods before Me, do not murder, do not commit adultery, etc. . . . *then* I will love you." See how it becomes something for something?

Diluting the Covenant

The problem with legalism is that it dilutes the covenant. An unconditional covenant has unconditional obligations. If I have loved you with an unconditional love, I have the right to demand unconditional loyalty.

But we could reverse the covenant and turn it inside out. Then, if you perform halfway, I'll perform halfway. If you perform not at all, then I will perform not at all.

Legalism is the subtlest way of all to get out of the covenant. It turns the covenant into a contract, assures the failure of the contract, and provides the rationale for the failure.

Legalism takes place in families when we say, "If you are good, if you do well in school, then we will respond to you." In marriage we turn the covenant into a contract when we make commitments based on our spouse's performance.

As a family therapist I am constantly running into people who define their relationships contractually. The contracts inevitably fail and become the excuse for the demise of the relationship. Legalism in families always ends in failure.

The obvious next step is to ask ourselves if we operate covenantally or contractually in our relationships.

The mother who began this book with us came to see herself as a first-class legalist. What resulted for her was the steady erosion of her closest relationships. When faced with her error, she went to those in her family and confessed her faults to them. Their first responses were predictable: They were glad Mom was finally going to get her act together.

Neither she nor I anticipated what eventually happened. The old habits didn't end easily. Those who had suffered the most because of the legalism became even greater legalists than she was. One by one, members of the family had to face their own inconsistencies and their contribution to the family's dysfunction. What had begun as a unanimous decision to send Mom for help ended with the demand that everybody get involved. The bottom line was that everybody contributed to the problem and then to the solution.

Theirs was a better home once they decided to live covenantly. Ironically, it demanded more work to live there. No one could slough off. Everybody had to contribute.

Covenants are rarely easier than contracts. In fact, sometimes in therapy we start a family out at the level of contract because that's the level at which they can perform. It takes a more sophisticated system to function covenantally.[5]

We are saved through faith and not works. The goal is to live together by faith and not works. It's one thing to say it; it's another to live it.

If you are a contractualist, the time to start living differently is now. If you are a legalist, admit it to yourself and to those you live with. Things go better when we live with one another according to the principle of covenant.

A Brief Summary

*The nature of covenant is unconditional commitment.
Implicit in every covenant is the certainty of betrayal.
Embedded in every act of covenant-promise is the reality of disillusionment, disobedience, and disheartenment.
*The nature of contract is something for something.
Contracts become destructive when they replace covenants in relationships that are meant to be covenantal.
*The dilemma becomes one of legalism.
Legalism occurs when rules and regulations must be followed in order to receive what should be unconditionally given in a covenantal relationship.

Gift Giving,
Gift Getting

One of my most delightful adult memories centers on children. For several summers I have served as the family speaker at Forest Home, a Christian conference center in the San Gabriel Mountains near Los Angeles.

Every Friday the children who are a part of the conference put on a parade. They come marching into the center of camp dressed in outfits relevant to the theme of the week.

On one occasion I complimented a four-year-old, "What a pretty flower you are."

"I'm not a flower," came his indignant reply. "I'm a lion!"

He marched on to join the rest of his cohorts, certain that the adult he had just encountered was blind if not totally stupid.

The children demonstrate such abandonment as they march to the "Disney on Parade" music. The whole event seems to embrace what it means to be a Christian; the children's exuberance, the parents' proud beaming as they take roll after roll of 35mm film. A delightfully innocent, frolicsome quality permeates the air.

It is no secret that such a sense of celebration is easier for some to express than for others. And some find it easy to give and get gifts. For others it is difficult.

In the same way, God's gift of life in Christ is easy for some to accept but hard for others. In this chapter we'll explore what makes receiving God's love easy or hard. A foundation is laid early in a child's life; it is the seedbed from which the ability to love God grows or from which the difficulty to love Him springs up.

The innocence of children and the teaching of Jesus

The last time I was at Forest Home I came away wondering when and where those children's innocence drains off to become the hardhearted realism or cynicism of the adult. What is it that provokes the change in you and me? Not that we would ever want to go back, but if only we could hold onto that openness mirrored in the children's faces.

The passage of Scripture that captures what I'm trying to describe is Matthew 18: 1-6. Jesus introduces the thought that Christian maturity is associated with the innocence possessed by a child. To us, innocence and maturity are often mutually exclusive. But to Him, they were vitally related. Hear His words:

> At that time the disciples came to Jesus, saying, "Who is the greatest in the kingdom of heaven?" And calling to him a child, he put him in the midst of them, and said, "Truly, I say to you, unless you turn and become like children, you will never enter the kingdom of heaven. Whoever humbles himself like this child, he is the greatest in the kingdom of heaven. Whoever receives one such child in my name receives me; but whoever causes one of these little ones who believe in me to sin, it would be better for him to have a great millstone fastened round his neck and to be drowned in the depth of the sea" (RSV).

Two things about this passage stand out in bold relief to me. The first is the attitude of the child and Christ's use of it as a metaphor of the Christian life. How astounding that the presumptuous innocence of a child is held up as a measure of faith. Jesus lauds the capacity of children to believe that of course God is a loving Father who delights in taking care of them; that all of creation has been put here for them; that because God has given so much to them it only makes sense that they should give themselves back to Him. To them, all of life is synchronous; it all fits together. There is nothing or nowhere that God doesn't belong.

The second issue that stands out to me deals with those who abuse children. The frightening conclusion from the passage is that God places His highest priority on the welfare of children and their innocence. When they are violated, something of His kingdom is defaced. Evidently the loss is so irretrievable that only the most horrible repositories are fit for the abusers. His words are sufficiently solemn to give us all reason to take heed.

Patterns of parenting: kinds of children

We return to the question, What turns the innocence of a child into the cynicism of the adult? I'd like to cast the issue into another light. It has to do with the nature of the parent/child relationship.

Through research we know, or at least have a strong suspicion, that how we were raised as children and how we related to our fathers and mothers have a strong influence on how we perceive God.[1]

For example, when we say the Lord's Prayer, "Our Father which art in Heaven . . .," the word "Father" will conjure up within us an image much like our earthly father or mother.

For some, that image is positive because the relationship they had with their earthly parents was positive. Others, however, are not so fortunate. Not all of us were raised by parents who took as their parental model the Biblical injunctions to raise their children "in the discipline and instruction of the Lord" (Eph. 6: 4, RSV). I know of Christians who cannot pray to God the Father because to do so provokes terrible, abusive memories.

These children-now-adults are more likely to live contractually rather than covenantally. They are likely to find it difficult to live by grace and to freely receive God's gifts. Though Christians, they often miss the joy and freedom of the Christian life. Life is all work and little play; the Christian life is no different.

Let me suggest five kinds of children, who, when they grow up, experience difficulty accepting the grace of God and/or living graciously with others.

The Abused Child

Current research on family violence indicates that on the national average as many as one in four children experiences significant ongoing abuse in the family of origin.[2] Similarly, a recent study in Los Angeles indicated that as many as one in four young girls has been involved in some incestuous relationship with a father, stepfather, brother, or cousin.[3] The increase in incest is frightening and is reaching epidemic proportions.

What effect does abuse have on a child, both in the short- and in the long-term? In the short-term, the child is more likely to experience difficulty in school, to suffer both physical and emotional illness, and to function at a level far below potential. Abuse debilitates.

In the long-term, the effects of abuse are more difficult to categorize. Logic tells us that the child would find it difficult to trust, to establish healthy permanent relationships, and to function at full potential in the adult world.

In terms of the child's relationship with God, abuse takes its toll as well. The abused child grows up with a parent-figure who is like a big fist, someone who takes the child's innocence and acts violently against it. There is a natural instinct in that child-now-adult to cringe at the mention of a parent. The child comes to believe that God, like a parent-figure, is an instrument of punishment; that He is not one who stands with arms open wide but one who represents judgment.

Abused children carry inside themselves a sense of dread.

Nothing is going to work out for them. God the Father, the Heavenly Parent, is out to get them. Sometimes they can be suspicious to the point of paranoia.

"I know you say that God loves me. I'll just wait and see," abused children-turned-adults say.

As they begin to unravel and tug at their feelings, they often find that beneath their fears of God are fears of parents. Obviously they fear physical violence.

They also fear symbolic violence. Their parents may not have hit or spanked or physically abused them. Rather, children were faced with parents who lost control of themselves verbally. Many, many adults have memories of parents screaming violently. Now, in their adult world, the children cannot bear to have people raise their voices at them.

I remember being with a couple who were in the midst of an argument. He raised his voice, and she flinched.

She said, "Don't yell."

He said, "I'm not yelling."

She replied, "Yes, you are yelling."

He turned to me and asked my opinion. It didn't sound to me as if he were yelling, but that was irrelevant. To her he was. Later as we talked, it surfaced that she was an abused child. She emotionally believed that as voices began to rise, violence was just around the corner.

The abused child-now-adult comes to Scripture and psychologically underlines all of the "woe" passages. Dread and judgment are to be expected. Joy and acceptance are not. Survival, not happiness, is the issue. Life is seen as a day-to-day experience rather than with a sense of anticipation. He or she struggles with hope because hope requires looking forward to tomorrow, but tomorrow is always bleak.

The Neglected Child

The second pattern in childhood doesn't involve abuse or violence. Rather, neglected children-now-adults have a sense of growing up on their own.[4]

The classic example of the neglected child is the child of

the alcoholic parent. He or she grows up realizing that the parents cannot be depended upon for anything; that the child has got to make it on his or her own in the world. As a result, the child often develops a kind of hyperindependence. He or she normally doesn't feel accountable to anyone because there was no one to be accountable to in the past. The child tends to go on alone.

Through the years I have interacted with the children of professional Christian leaders and workers, I've been struck with the number of children-now-adults who remember their earliest days as days of deprivation. Mom or Dad just were never there. The children grew up like weeds in a garden, with a randomness about their lives.

Like the abused child, but for different reasons, the neglected child-now-adult finds it difficult to trust. That child remembers promises that were made and broken.

"Sure, I'll come to your open house," his parent promises. "What time do I need to be there?" (Maybe this time he'll make it.)

The child works feverishly at school getting ready.

Then comes the big evening. His classroom is filled with activity. Children and their parents mill around like the ants who make up one of the displays. An hour passes, then two.

Reluctantly the child realizes that the hoped-for parent isn't going to show. The child looks around the room and counts the fathers and mothers who did make it.

He chokes back the tears of disappointment and goes on with his life, making excuses to the other children as to why his parents couldn't come. Inside he knows the "truth."

The child believes they didn't come because they don't care. Soon, the child learns not to care. He carries on without an emotional connectedness with the parent(s). He shields himself from caring as a means of protecting himself from disappointment.

When he grows up and hears the words of Jesus, "Lo, I am with you always, to the close of the age" (Mt. 28: 20, RSV), he says, "I'll bet. You can't expect anyone to be there when you want or need him to be, even God. You have to take care of yourself because no one else will."

The Pampered Child

Our third dysfunctional pattern is the parenting style that produces the pampered child. This is the child who, when growing up, is showered with attention. All he or she has to do is make the slightest sound, and Mommy and Daddy are there. Very often the pampered child is the focal point of the child-centered family. Mom and Dad focus on the child because their marriage is barren.

Christmas can be an embarrassment, with so many gifts for the child that it borders on the ludicrous. The child comes to expect that he or she is the center of the universe and that special events always revolve around that center.

The irony of it all is that many times the pampered child is raised by a neglected and deprived child-now-adult. Somewhere in the past the neglected child said, "When I grow up and have children of my own, I'll be there whenever my child needs me. I'll give her gifts, and whenever she has a need, I'll be there." The problem arises when the neglected child-become-parent goes too far with too much.

Pampered children grow up with too little discipline and control rather than too little love. They learn to throw tantrums when they want something, knowing they can intimidate their parents into giving them what they want. They are spoiled.

When they grow up, they tend to chronically suffer from lack of self-discipline. They find it difficult to say no to themselves. They are vulnerable to self-indulgence and lethargy. They struggle with maintaining motivation.

In their relationship with God, they transfer their parental expectations to God. They expect God to come running whenever they want. They prejudicially read the verses in the New Testament offering abundant life. They unconsciously screen out the verses that have implicit within them the demands of self-denial and sacrifice.

"What's in it for me?" is their query. "What has God done for me lately?" is their quest. The Gospel becomes a "gimme" Gospel, and when tough times come, they are vulnerable to falling away.

"I thought Christianity was supposed to mean living high off the hog," they grumble, "and all I'm doing is groveling in the dirt. If that's all there is, then forget it."

Pampered children grow up to be pampered Christians, expecting others to take care of them; expecting God to do the pampering, or the church, or the spouse. They can be very hard to live with; they can drain the resources from the most resilient marriage or the most giving church.

Perhaps the greatest difficulty is that pampered children rarely are willing to admit that they were pampered. When it is suggested, usually by their spouse, they resist vehemently. The way they were raised is the way you're supposed to raise children. That they were indulged is often a blind spot.

The pampered child is one of the most destructive parenting patterns because it is so difficult to face and to change.

The Parentified Child

This pattern has been identified by the family theorist, Ivan Nagy.[6] It operates at what Nagy calls the contextual or ethical level; thus, it is rarely conscious.

The parentified child develops when the child is expected to compensate one or both of the parents for the deprivations of the parent's own childhood. In one sense the parents have received a bill because *their* parents were deprived. Rather than change the grandparents, the bill comes due for the child. The dynamics are generational, with the youngest generation compensating their parents for the losses accrued when the parent(s) were children. In plain terms, the child grows up with the sense of being responsible for taking care of his or her parent(s). The child parents the parent.

My mother and I have talked and have come to the conclusion that I fit into this category. My father died when I was seven. My mom tells the story of his return from North Africa following the Second World War. He had been home for about two weeks when he called me into the bedroom where he was resting on the bed with my mother. My father said to me, a seven-year-old, "Denny, if something happens to me, I want you to take care of your mother." Evidently he had a premonition of his death. A day or so later he left, and a week later he was dead from a heart attack.

About eight years later, when I was 15, I was awakened by my mother. My grandfather was on the living room sofa dying. He, too, had suffered a heart attack. The ambulance had been called, and the family had gathered in hushed conversation waiting for its arrival. He beckoned me to his side and said, "Denny, I'm dying. I want you to take care of your mother and your grandma." They were the last words he spoke before he died. By the time the ambulance arrived, he was gone.

"Denny, take care of your mother." The same words twice spoken. Needless to say, I grew up thinking and feeling that I was responsible for her. My task was to parent my parent. I missed something of my own childhood: the freedom to live with childish abandon.

It wasn't until I had became a Christian, was married, and my wife had a big, healthy, happy child inside her that I was able to reach down inside myself and find that there was a child inside me, too. I'd never flown a kite until I flew one with my wife. "Dennis, lighten up!" was her constant cry during those early years. It was hard for me then to have fun for fun's sake, and it still is.

I'd never experienced what it means to be a child until I experienced it in my own children. All of that was new. I was busy being responsible for my mother, my wife, my children, the church, and even God. I realized that as a parentified child I was even taking care of God.

Parentified children are infused with responsibility. If something or someone needs to be taken care of, they'll do it. The difficulty arises when they need to be taken care of. Their tendency is to deny their own needs or shield those closest to them from the reality of their pain. Parentified children are not supposed to hurt; they are supposed to give comfort to others, not need comfort themselves.

In terms of the Christian life, the parentified child-become-adult struggles with the *work* of being a Christian because he or she doesn't experience the joy of play. Responsibility comes easy but rest doesn't. These children easily burn out. The side of the road of Christian service is strewn with the weary bodies of parentified children. Like rusting tanks on a forgotten and distant battlefield, parentified children who have overdosed on responsibility occupy themselves with recovering from nervous breakdowns or debilitating physical illness. While recovering, they feel guilty that they are immobile and out of service. The church, in response, wonders when they will be back in harness. Such is the dilemma of the parentified child: There is always more to do and others to be responsible for.

Their dilemma can be answered by allowing others to be responsible, to remember that the world doesn't rest on their shoulders.

Recently, I had to laugh at myself. My wife Lucy and I were in Wheaton visiting our oldest daughter. For the life of me I couldn't get my directions right. Every time I tried to drive out of town I would turn the wrong way and head us off in the wrong direction. I was supposed to be the "responsible one." With some difficulty I eventually handed the map to Lucy and abandonded my need to navigate. To my relief, she navigated us very well. We got to where we needed to get, and I was none the worse for wear.

The parentified child in me needed to learn that lesson. Others *can* take responsibility for life and the tasks of ministry. The difficulty is in letting go.

The Controlling Child

The last pattern we'll mention is the controlling child.[7] These children are classics. They are usually older daughters who were given the task of parenting their siblings. They become the world's mother hens. They take care of others by being the ever-present nurturer and comfort-giver. Like the parentified child, they miss much of their own childhood; they miss the privilege of being cared for themselves.

They are the bosses of the world—nurturing bosses—but still bosses. They need to be in control. They are good at telling the world, and even God, what to do. Their motto is:

"Let me tell you what to do and how to do it." Martha, in the New Testament, is their patron saint.

But, who takes care of the Marthas, the controlling children, of the world? Who gives to them? Who does the work when they are tired? Families who have a Martha as a mother become spoiled. She does the work—often at the cost of her resentment—but she still does the work.

Again, the church has relied on the hardworking backs of controlling children. Where would we be without them? When the doors open, you can count on their being there. If there is a task to be done, give it to the controlling children. They have adapted all of their lives, and they will adapt again. We would not be where we are today in the church or in our families were it not for the controlling children.

Eventually, they, too, burn out. They are consumed with the ache of their unappreciated feelings. They weary at taking care of others and wish to be taken care of. Unfortunately, all too often the family and the church doesn't hear them because we need them.

Work with no rest afflicts controlling children's relationships with God as well. They can weary of being Christians because they are so earnest in their approach to the Christian life. However, when God's grace comes to them wrapped in the care and concern of a spouse, a child, or a friend, they can be deeply appreciative. Sometimes, if they let themselves, they can recoup the loss of their own childhood nurture through the ministry of being nurtured by others. It will happen only if they let it.

Who are the grown-ups?

Jesus draws all children onto His lap and comforts them. The kingdom of God has a place for them all and in some ways is like them all. The abused with their fears, the neglected with their resentment, the pampered with their narcissism, the parentified with their responsibility, and the controlling with their compulsive work.

God's grace doesn't require that they be perfect before they can bring their troubled pasts to Him. He is accustomed to healing the lame and the crippled. Those who are whole don't need it.

It is God *the Father* who has loved us with unremitting, covenantal love. It is the same Father who has declared us accepted in the beloved. However twisted our past, we are whole in Him. Jesus does love the little children. To the list of "red, brown, yellow, black, and white," we can add the abused, the neglected, the pampered, the parentified, and the controlling. It is good to be reminded that they are, indeed, precious in His sight.

A Brief Summary

*The innocence of children and the teaching of Jesus.
  Jesus lauds the innocence of children.
  When that innocence is violated, God's kingdom is defaced.
*Patterns of parenting: Kinds of children.
  Types of children who have difficulty accepting God's gifts:
  1) The abused child. The child who experiences verbal or physical abuse.
  2) The neglected child. The child who grows up on his or her own.
  3) The pampered child. The child who is showered with attention.
  4) The parentified child. The child who feels responsible to care for his or her parent(s).
  5) The controlling child. The child who feels he or she must nurture and comfort others.
*Who are the grown-ups? All the types of children, whom God loves with covenantal love.

Parents:
The Memory
Makers

When Lucy was pregnant with our first baby, it didn't really hit me that I was going to be a father until the fetus began to move and I could feel the movement. Then came the birth. It was an exciting time. We went to the hospital late at night, and by the next morning our first child had been born.

I visited Lucy in the recovery room, and we both celebrated the event. Though drowsy from the anesthetic, she was pleased and so was I. I passed by the nurses' station on my way out of the hospital, and the charge-nurse asked, "How is Mrs. Guernsey doing?"

"Fine," I replied. "She had an easy time of it."

The nurse rose menacingly from her chair. "Young man," she threatened, "it may have been quick, but it's never easy, and don't you forget it."

Appropriately chastened, I walked to my car thinking about how naive I was. If I were that dense about the birth process, what kind of parent would I be?

Three weeks later Lucy developed a severe staph infection that proved to be life-threatening. It required hospitalization, surgery, and months of recuperation. Much of the time she ran a high fever and struggled to stay alive, all the while trying to take care of her new baby.

During that time much of the care of our newborn fell to me. She would direct me from her bed, and I would perform the needed tasks as best I could.

I was involved in parenting up to my unprepared ears. Often it felt as though I was in over my head. But with the help of my mother and my 12-year-old sister-in-law, we made it. We were launched into the parenting journey.

Parenting is an awesome task, one for which most of us are unprepared and ill-trained. It's no wonder that we sometimes bungle the job. Somehow we muddle through, and our children grow up in spite of us, it seems. Yet the society that demands we be perfect in raising our children turns around and provides us with little training to do the job. The expectations are greater than the average person can fulfill.

Layered on top of the problem of inadequate socialization is the problem of uncontrollable circumstances. Who can foresee the times of illness, the demands of careers, the loss of jobs, the trauma of death?

Whatever happens, we must go on. The baby must still be bathed and fed. The children must be disciplined and put to bed at a decent hour. The money must be earned to pay for the basics of life.

It all affects the job we do as parents. It is a very demanding process. The danger for authors like myself is to make it seem easier than it really is.

If all of this is true, it seems to me that the best place to begin this chapter is with a comment on God's grace. Nowhere is grace and forgiveness more needed than in the parenting process. There are no perfect people here, only strugglers.

But the fear and anxiety that infuses parents today is more deadly than the mistakes of parenting. We create more problems for ourselves because we constantly focus on the problems. We don't launch into the process knowing that we will make mistakes and, thus, deal with ourselves with a measure of mercy and forgiveness.

Such is the danger latent in the previous chapter. It is all too easy to identify with all of the dysfunctional patterns. One woman came up to me at a recent conference and pleaded for help because she saw herself in every one of the problems that was described. How can we release ourselves from the terrible guilt and burden that weighs us down when we are so conscious of our mistakes and faults as parents?

The philosophy of parenting Lucy and I follow proves helpful at this point: Good parents are responsible for building memories for their children.

Thus, the primary task of parents is to provide more good memories than bad. The onus of perfection is removed. The job is simplified. We are memory makers. Wherever and however we can, we are to create an environment in which the child is able to grow himself up.[1]

The issue of more good memories than bad ones helps us to face reality. It is impossible to fill a child's life with only good memories; life doesn't unfold that way. Do the best that you can and trust God to make sense of both your successes and your failures. As Christians, we need to remember that God is as concerned about our children as we are. We can deal with our anxiety if we trust Him to be a part of the process.

With this in mind, I would like to divide the parenting process into two parts. The first is the "what," or the content of parenting, and the second, covered in the next chapter, is the "how," or the context for parenting.[2]

The psychologist Erik Erikson has influenced modern thinking about human development more than any other contemporary writer.[3] He successfully brought to the attention of psychological theorists the developmental tasks of the individual, beginning with the child and ending with the mature adult. When I think of the content of parenting, I think of Erikson's categories. What follows is my adaptation of his theory.

The task of attachment

Human infants are totally dependent. They cannot care for themselves and must rely on their parents for everything. They are physically and emotionally more helpless for a longer time than any other creature created by God. Because of this dependency, they are vulnerable to feelings of frustration and anxiety from birth. It's easy to forget that infants and young children have feelings because, as adults, our feelings are tied to our ability to verbalize them. But feelings are preverbal. Babies know how we feel about them. We don't know how they know, but we know that they do.

The first task of the parent, therefore, is to establish a kind of security for the child, a special connectedness. When the infant was *en utero*, the attachment was literal. The baby was connected by means of an umbilical cord. At birth that connection is severed. The trauma of birth and the nakedness of life are enough to strike fear into the heart of the child. He or she cannot be shielded from nakedness, but the child can be reassured. Reassurance results when the child is made to feel loved and wanted.

Much of the anxiety of childhood and the subsequent anxiety of adulthood stems from the failure to bond or attach during infancy. The stakes are indeed high. The ability to trust is established very early.

The profound simplicity of the task belies its importance. "I love you. I want you. You belong" are words easily spoken.

But words are not enough for children; they must be backed with actions. Loving, wanting, and including are not just feelings. They are actions, and children know more based on what we do than on what we say.

Parenthetically, let me say that it's never too late to say the words or demonstrate them through actions. However misparented children may seem to be, healing can take place. The parent needs to acknowledge failure and make a genuine attempt to love the child, to assert that the child is wanted and to make a place for the child so that he or she belongs. The only thing that gets in the way is our pride and our resistance to say, "I've been wrong."

The child's ability to trust is the first goal of parenting. It develops through steady, consistent, caring behavior that can be known by even the preverbal child. Caring is expressed through words and actions that say, "You are loved. You are wanted. You belong."

The task of identification

The second content task of parenting consists of developing the identity of the child. In the very young child of one to three, it begins with the parents walking the tightrope between encouraging the child's autonomy and establishing parental control. Erikson labels the child who is over-controlled at this age as suffering from doubt. The child wonders whether he or she can move about in the world without bringing the constant disapproval of the parent.

In the four- and five-year-old, the question of initiative arises: Can the child be free to explore the world and thus discover who he or she is?

In the day-to-day world of the parent this means allowing the child to make a mess as he or she plays at being an adult. The child is practicing being a person. Often the child is trying out what it feels like to be "just like you."

The last issue during the stage of identification is industry. The six- to eleven-year-old is busy becoming an adult. Can the child try new skills without the parent's criticism? Can he or she "fail" without the parent's displeasure? During this stage the child learns how to work and to take initiative, how to launch out into the world and to try new things. The child practices how to function adequately in an adult world that requires creativity, adaptability, and flexibility.

During the stage of identification, the child finds out who he or she is. The parents' responses resemble a mirror. The child's self-image is determined by how he or she comes to see his or her self reflected in the responses of significant others.

At this stage, in addition to self-image, maleness or female-ness is established during this stage. Does the child like himself or herself as a boy or a girl? Many parents believe that children's gender comfort is established during the teenage years when they begin to think obsessively about the oppo-site sex. But, by the time that happens, the decision has already been made.

The task of differentiation

The critical issue during the teenage years is independence. Is it possible to progressively release the child-now-teenager into the world to function independently?

The tendency of many Christian parents during this stage is to bind children and tie them to the home for fear they will be overcome by the world. If the parents think and feel that they have not done a good job preparing their child for the adult world, then the threat of the teenager's freedom is overwhelming. If the child is not ready to accept responsibility for managing self and conduct, then the parents are placed in a double bind. On the one hand, they face the prospect of a teenager who will run amuck with freedom. On the other, they face the prospect of a resentful and rebellious monster prowling the house, aching for a fight.

This issue is of such import that I'll spend two chapters later in the book dealing with it.

The task of generalization

The last content issue of effective parenting is helping the teenager/young adult develop the ability to establish healthy intimate relationships.

The agenda for this stage involves the modeling of appropriate and comfortable intimacy on the part of the parents themselves. By this time, most of what parents can do for their offspring has been done.

Do they see in their parent(s) the ability to be vulnerable and nurturing toward others? Can they believe that community, the interdependence with others, is possible? Do they have a sense of healthy responsibility for their neighbor? Do they have a Christian world view that lifts their sense of self beyond the boundaries of their immediate context? Can they become "world Christians"?

The logical progression is to move from the dependence of the child to the independence of the teenager/young adult to the interdependence of the adult years. Each stage is necessary. Each is preamble for the next.

The goal is to come to the place where the person is able to live with the tension between individual freedom and responsibility to the community, whether that community be immediate family, the church, or the world. For the parent, the goal is to remember that perfection will not be achieved in the parenting process. There will be mistakes along the way. The parent will stumble and sometimes even fall. But in each stage of the child's development, the parent strives to create good memories. Enough good memories to outweigh the bad. And *that* task is achievable.

A Brief Summary

The content (or "what") of parenting includes:
*The task of attachment.
  This task includes communicating to the child, "You are loved. You are wanted. You belong."
*The task of identification.
  During this era, the child develops self-image and gender comfort.
*The task of differentiation.
  This includes releasing the teen into the world.
*The task of generalization.
  Modeling the interdependence of adulthood is the parents' role in this, the last task.

It's in the Packaging

I remember reading in a national magazine about a brand-name product that was easily the best on the market, but no one was buying it. Subsequent market research indicated that the content was detracted from by the packaging. The manufacturers had failed to recognize that packaging forms a symbolic and connecting relationship between the product and the consumer. When they changed the package and made it more attractive, the public responded and bought the product at a rate the manufacturers couldn't keep up with.

The same equation holds true with parenting. No matter how pure the motives and Christian the intent, if a parent neglects the packaging of the content, the content itself will be rejected by the child. "How" precedes the "what" or the "what" is quashed.

Let me suggest four "contexts," or relational packages, that enhance the parenting content we discussed in the last chapter.

The context of nurture and support

I am not a farmer nor am I the son of a farmer, but I have learned one thing. If you don't take care of your crops. you'll not reap what you want; you'll reap your neglect. Now. I can grow weeds. My garden for the past two years has vacillated between healthy vegetables and healthy weeds. Of course, I know that my gardening habits are what do me in. I garden in binges; I'm not consistent. The trees and plants that make up my backyard suffer from my neglect. As a result, I spend much of my time repairing the damage.

Child-rearing is no different. Children need steady, unglamorous nurture and support.

By nurture I mean the provision of needs that are physical, emotional, and spiritual. When we make the decision to have children, we have already made the choice to limit our freedom as adults. In that sense, children are demanding by reason of their existence. Because they "are," they must be cared for. The needs of children begin at the most basic level of food and clothing and become more elaborate as they grow older. What they need to know is that their needs will be dealt with competently and fairly. Nurture is best if it just seems to happen.

By support I mean the ability to communicate felt-love to the child. To be there when you're needed. Even to be there when you're wanted. Most of all, just to be there.

When I was in high school, I played football. I can remember a friend whose father came around at practice and just stood on the sidelines and watched. The father would be in the stands whether our game was at home or away. I recall how impressed I was that that father was so supportive. As my friend and I talked, it became obvious that his relationship with his father was something special to him.

Years later I bumped into my friend at a local Sunday school convention. I had become a Christian since the last time I had seen him. We reminisced, and I mentioned my memories of his father. Much to my amazement, he informed me that his father had been a successful pastor of a growing church at the time, and that he had intentionally worked his schedule around so that he could be there when his son played football.

No Excuse

This was in stark contrast to the tales my pastor friends and I were telling each other about our schedules. We just didn't have time for our families; the demands were too great. Quietly, inside, I knew that I was only making excuses. My family and my ministry could both be served, but it would take deliberate and concerted effort on my part.

I don't have sons who play football, but my daughters have participated in gymnastics and have played soccer. They have been in drama and have engaged in extracurricular activities in high school. With my wife's steady encouragement, I have managed to attend most of my daughters' special events. It takes work and planning on my part, but it's worth it to see my daughter's face light up when she sees us in the crowd. She knows that we support her and that we're behind her.

Nurture and support are like investments we make in our parenting future. Inevitably when crises come—and they most certainly will—the context of nurture and support becomes the boundary within which we work out our differences. It's hard for teenagers to say, "You don't care" if they have received consistent nurture and support. They may say, "You don't understand," but they'll probably never point out, "You don't care." In today's hectic world, nurture and support no longer happen easily. They must be planned.

The context of comfort

Comfort is the human response to another's pain. When we parent our children, we need to remember that every child's pain is the worst. There is no such thing as a hierarchy of hurt. Sometimes people try to comfort others in a crazy kind of way by discounting their pain or by casting it into some kind of contrast with another's hurt. The results can be bizarre.

The time I hurt the most was when our oldest child, a son, died at age four. The grief seemed more than Lucy or I could bear.

One woman in our church came up to me and tried to

comfort me. "I know you hurt," she said. "But my pain is worse. My son died when he was 18. We had him all those many more years to love."

Several weeks later, another woman approached me with a similar tale. "I know you hurt, but my pain is worse." I shuddered at what was to come. "My child was stillborn. You at least had your son for four and one-half years. I didn't have mine for a single day."

A Hierarchy of Hurt

Looking back on that experience, I now realize that both women were trying to comfort themselves rather than bring comfort to me. They did so by creating a system in which one person's loss is greater or lesser than another's.

I'm convinced it doesn't work that way. When it comes to loss, the natural human response is to grieve. When it comes to pain, the human response is to hurt. Whether it is the loss of a tooth or the loss of a hamster or the loss of a job or the loss of a child, the natural response is to grieve and hurt.

Some parents respond to their children's pain by using it as an opportunity to teach them to be tough. "Suck it up and tough it out," says the drill-instructor type of father. "I told you you'd hurt yourself," says the less strident but equally uncomforting mother.

Both seize on the moment to teach their child a lesson rather than to respond comfortingly to the child's pain. They teach their child to deny the pain through their parents' denial of it. "Tough" becomes the negation of feelings. "I told you so" is the subtle denial of the child's personhood. Both are destructive in the long run.

Why do some people find it difficult to give comfort? I'm convinced that if there was a deficit in comfort-receiving when you're a child, it's very difficult to be a comfort-giver when you're an adult. When I hear hard-nosed people, either male or female, say, "You've made your bed, now lie in it," my instincts tell me that when they were children in need of comfort someone failed to give it. Now they are passing the dysfunction on to their children.

To give comfort is to participate in the work of the Holy Spirit, who is the greatest Comforter of all. To give comfort is to participate in the healing process established by God the Father, who took the wandering and hurting nation of Israel up into His arms with "cords of compassion" (Hos. 11: 1-4). To comfort is to emulate the Lord Jesus, who recognized Peter's pain and humiliation and who reached out to him in forgiveness. The giving of comfort is both godly and good.

The context of discipline

Discipline entails the setting and enforcing of boundaries. It is saying no in such a way that children learn to say no to themselves. Most of us want what we want *now*. Self-discipline in the child is the goal of healthy parental discipline. The trick is not to defeat your goal by the way you handle the situation.

Several years ago we took a 12-year-old foster son into our home for almost two years. When he was a small child, he had been severely abused and deprived. We'll call him Jim.

By the time he got to us he had developed several negative habits and attitudes. Initially Jim was warm, responsive, cooperative, and effusive. He couldn't help enough. But three or so months into our experience with him, he became much like his usual self: sometimes cooperative, but more often than not resentful and rebellious.

We had always used corporal (physical) discipline in our home with our three children, and it seemed to have worked with them. They were fairly decent, easy-to-get-along-with children. However, in the State of California, it is illegal to spank a foster child. We had to find another way to control and discipline our boy.

Learning to Demand

How do you get a tough, resentful kid to do what you want him to do? We learned the meaning of a "new" word, the word "demand."

It's fairly common for parents to unconsciously give a child the option not to do what they want him to do. "If you don't do thus-and-so, I'll do thus-and-so." The statement invites, or at least holds out to the child, the option not to do what you want. If he's willing to suffer the consequences, he doesn't have to do what he's told.

Jim had learned to defeat all comers by his willingness to accept the consequences of his resistance. He just didn't care. If you hit him, you proved his opinion of adults to be true—they were violent and abusive. If you tried to bribe him, you were weak and could be manipulated. If you used punitive means, you would defeat whatever goals you had for Jim, however valid and useful those goals might be.

The Battle of the Wills

The issue with us was one of a conflict of wills. Because Jim was single-minded, he usually won out. We had to find another way. We demanded. "You *will* do what we tell you to do, period. There is no other choice. We'll not lose control; we'll not quit; we'll stay with it until you do what you're told."

The particular line that we drew with Jim had to do with his schoolwork. To him a "C" was outstanding work.

He brought home an assignment having to do with "Tobacco, Alcohol, and Drugs." He assumed that, as before, he would just not do it. We decided he would. We demanded that he do it.

"You're going to sit here and work on your project until it's finished," we demanded. He would show us. Six hours later we were still sitting with him at the kitchen table.

"I'm tired," he whined.

"That's too bad. You're not done, so you'll just have to sit here until you finish." We were determined.

Very late that evening we told him he could go to bed, but when he came home from school the next day, we would be there, and he would be expected to work on his report.

The next day Lucy met Jim at the door and escorted him to the kitchen table. He stayed there until dinner. After dinner I joined him, and he continued to sit defiantly.

"As soon as you do some work you can go to bed," I said.

Five or so hours later he went to bed with three pages done. There was much more to do.

The third day Lucy met him at the door again. Six hours later he was beginning to crumble.

"All right!" he yelled. "I'll do your stupid report." (I let the distortion pass. I also didn't worry about his attitude. It didn't matter. What mattered was that he was doing his work.)

Angrily Jim wrote the final paragraphs of his report. When he was through, he dramatically flung his pencil on the table and stomped off to bed.

The approximately 18-hour ordeal was over. Our motto became, "The twig will bend before the branch will break." We had not broken either by giving in or by losing control. He had bent.

For the first time Jim turned in a homework assignment. When he got it back from his teacher, he proudly showed us the "B +" he had received. As he walked away to his room, we knew that we had prevailed.

There were more battles to come, but a tone had been set. We had *demanded* that he obey. Eventually he had no other choice. Our stubbornness had outlasted his.

I have included this example because I believe parents, especially Christian parents, rely too heavily on corporal discipline. While I realize the Scripture counsels us to not "spare the rod," common sense tells us that there comes a time when we need to have other models of discipline available to us.

Whether it takes the form of behavioral modification, natural consequences, or the use of demand, the method is ultimately irrelevant. What is of greater significance is that we find a system of discipline that works for us and that preserves the integrity and personhood of the child.

Discipline is like pruning a tree. Prune too little, and the tree grows haphazardly. Prune too much, and the tree's growth is stunted and permanent damage results. Somewhere in the middle is the golden mean, the place where discipline is a stimulant to growth rather than an inhibition.

Again, discipline is a godly good. "The Lord disciplines him whom he loves" (Heb. 12: 6, RSV). It is a necessary ingredient in the establishment of an effective context for parenting.

The context of effective communication

Remember our discussion on communication and metacommunication? The former deals with the content of the message; the latter deals with how the message is sent. In terms of effective parenting, communication sets the tone for the relationship, but I would like to make some comments on the process, the metacommunication, itself.

First, the place to begin modeling good communication is not only with your child but also with your spouse. It is the marriage that made the child, and it is the marriage that grows the child. By this I mean, the relationship between the child's parents is dominant in the child's process of learning to communicate with others.

This is true even for single-parent families. The way in which parents communicate during and after a divorce strongly affects how children communicate with their parents and with each other. How can we expect children to function better than they see the significant adults in their lives functioning?

Second, good communication involves sending clear, unambiguous messages. Adults sometimes are captured by poor habits. Cynicism, sarcasm, and even teasing can dull and inhibit the parenting process.

Suppose you're concerned with your son's or daughter's weight. As he or she walks out of the kitchen, brownie in hand, you say sarcastically, "Still on the ole diet, I see." The eyes fill with resentment. The content issue, your concern about weight, is lost in the meta-issue of your sarcasm. Predictably, the child doesn't respond. He or she walks off sullenly to safer confines.

Do you say what you mean, or do you mask your intentions in the way you say it? It's good to begin a statement that might be misunderstood with a preamble, stating clearly your intentions.

For example, let's say you're concerned about your teenager's recent grade in algebra, and you anticipate the youth will become defensive merely at the mention of it. Begin your conversation with a short statement of intention: "I'm going to say something that could easily turn into a hassle. But I don't want to start a fight, and I certainly don't intend to come across as critical of you in general. But I am concerned with your grade in algebra."

If you need to say something, but you're not sure that you can say it right, say so. Be out on top of the table about it. It's better to declare clearly your motives and intentions than it is to be misunderstood.

The same process holds true if you want to underline what you're going to say because you really mean it. Rather than yell (the usual method of emphasis), say something to the effect: "What I'm going to say cannot be said with the kind of emotion I feel. In the past I've said things to you, and it seems like you don't hear. I want you to hear this, and I want you to remember it. I'm not yelling outside, but inside I am." Then comes the message, underlined and in capital letters.

62

Clear messages include clear and unambiguous intent as well as content.

He Who Has Ears . . .

The last meta-issue in communication that I would like to highlight is listening. Sometimes we fail to listen because we are in the habit of allowing ourselves to be distracted, to focus our attention on something besides the person who is speaking to us. At other times, we are too rigid and unwilling to yield. Why listen when you've already made up your mind?

In James's letter he describes the "wisdom from above," pointing out that one characteristic of the wise person is that he is "open to reason" (3: 17, RSV). The Amplified uses the phrase "[willing to] yield to reason."

There is a healthy *quid pro quo* involved here. If I give something away to my children, they'll give something to me in return. If I give them the right to be heard, they will give me the right to decide. In this sense, a family is a representative democracy. If the representatives listen to the people, the people will accept the decisions that are made, even if they don't like the decisions. The process requires that the people be heard.

Children both need and want to be heard. They too often think—and are told by our contemporary culture—that adults won't listen to them. They begin with the assumption that they won't be heard.

Listening = Obedience

The phenomenon of listening is at the heart of a critical matter for Christian parents: the issue of obedience. As Christian parents, we recognize the need for our children to learn obedience. But often they learn the opposite.

The etymology of the Greek word "to obey" provides a clue to the problem. The root of the word "obey" in the Greek New Testament is "to listen." It is the same root that we find in "acoustic," such as acoustic guitars or acoustic ceilings. To obey means to listen and respond. How can we get them to listen? Probably they will listen if they have been listened to. In this sense, listening is a vital dimension in the context of parenting.

Parents usually respond at this point with fear—what if they become permissive and compliant? Admittedly I risk being a soft touch and a pushover. But the greater issue to me is hearing and being heard. I'm willing to trade an occasional incident in which I am manipulated for the time when the chips are down and my children listen to what I have to say and respond appropriately. In covenant families, the family members hear and are heard by one another.

The context of celebration

In the closing months of the Vietnam War, I visited South Vietnam on business. I had gone to Saigon to arrange for the transfer of orphans from World Vision's child-care facilities to the agency I headed in Southern California.

As a part of my itinerary, I visited several orphanages. They were filled to their rafters with children, more than could be effectively cared for.

The sounds of war and the scars were everywhere. Most of the children who were there had known the direct, vicious effects of the war. They had seen their parents killed. They had known the terror of 120mm shelling.

Still they could play and laugh. You couldn't walk amongst them, sit and have them crawl on your lap, and not be touched with their spirit. Their unsophisticated play involved the use of sticks and twine and anything else they could lay their hands on.

For a while I stood on the second-floor balcony and watched the scene below. The clamor filled the courtyard; I'll never forget their laughter. They were the little children Jesus took on His lap and said the kingdom of Heaven was like them.

Outside on the streets of Saigon, the scene was dramatically different. Men and women scurried to and fro, knowing that the fall of the city was near. Public buildings were sandbagged and guarded by armed soldiers. Huge military vehicles thundered on the streets, honking their horns in warning to any and all in their path that they would stop for no one and nothing. There was no joy. There was no laughter. Adults were running that world.

Children understand the phenomenon of celebration. Adults forget. It's easy to become like Eore, the donkey in the Winnie the Poo stories. "The sun's out now, but soon there'll be clouds," he moans. Left to their own devices, adults will fill the sky with clouds.

What do I mean by celebration? It is raising children who, when they become adults, remember what it means to laugh, to enjoy life, and to play. Celebration involves keeping one's sense of humor. It involves encouraging an approach of wonderment toward the world, a curiosity, a spirit of inquiry. Most of all, it involves the maintenance of a playful and joyous attitude toward the world and toward God. It refuses to become moribund and defeated. Celebration brings the shout of the archangels and the sound of the trumpet out of the future and into the present tense. Celebration is the worship of God the Creator and the Giver of life and all good things.

Celebration is our response to Jesus' words: Except you come as little children, you can't know the kingdom of heaven (Mark 10: 15).

A Brief Summary

The context (or "how") of parenting includes:
*Nurture and support.
The parent provides for physical, emotional, and

spiritual needs, communicating felt-love to the child.
*Comfort.
The parent responds to the child's pain.
*Discipline.
The parent sets and enforces boundaries.
*Effective communication.
The parent models good communication with the
spouse. Each sends clear, unambiguous messages, and
each listens.
*Celebration.
Parents encourage children to retain their sense of
humor and wonderment toward the world even as they
become adults.

Good People Grow Prodigals, Too

In a Southern California church every Tuesday evening a small group of parents meets to pray and to provide one another with support. Each of these parents has a son or daughter whom we might label a prodigal. Every family represented has a loved one who has gone off into a far country.

Some have teenagers who have run away and are lost on the streets of Hollywood. Others have children who are into drugs or alcohol even though they haven't actually left home. Still others have sons or daughters who have dramatically rejected Christianity and are living life-styles in marked contrast to that of their parents.

Yet these parents represent the leadership of their church. They are deeply committed to Christ and rooted in the faith. They are men and women who raised their families as best they could according to what they knew at the time.

Several questions consistently surface as they take new members into their group. How could it happen to us? Didn't we do the best that we knew how? Don't we love God, and shouldn't that make a difference? Our children were in church from the time they were babies. They studied the Scriptures. They attended all of the youth camps. Why didn't all of that make a difference?

They are good people; they are conscientious parents. Yet their children are far off in another country. Sometimes their pain is more than they can bear, and they break down during the meeting and weep uncontrollably. There are no easy answers to their questions.

The veterans who have been in the group for years comfort the newcomers with words of patience. "Wait and trust God," they tell one another. "Forgive yourselves," they counsel their grieving colleagues. They have learned to "bear one another's burdens" (Gal. 6: 2, RSV). They understand the struggle and care that the other is hurting.[1]

One senior member of the group and a leader in the evangelical Christian world told me he had concluded that good people grow prodigals, too. Maturity as a Christian doesn't absolve you from the risk of having children reject Christ and a Christian life-style when they grow older. Parents must live with the choices of their offspring in the same way God lives with ours.

Some parents are in the midst of struggling with their prodigal. For other parents the problem seems threatening, like the impending thunderstorm on a hot and humid afternoon in the Midwest. You can see the clouds form and hear the thunder in the distance. You know that the wind and rain are coming; it's just a matter of time.

The story of the prodigal son as told by Jesus is the story of a covenant family. It's not the story of absolute and total success, but it's a story of relational dynamics like those I'm describing in this book.

I use the story as an example of a covenant family because it is used by Jesus as a metaphor of God's relationship with those who constitute His family. The father in the story is clearly meant by Jesus to represent the Heavenly Father. The prodigal son represents those who have wandered far from Him. The elder son typifies those who remain at home or in relationship with Him but who are bound and fettered by that relationship in an unhealthy way. The focus of the story is clearly on the waiting father, but the drama as it unfolds is descriptive of the families in the church mentioned above.

The Problem

From the perspective of a family therapist, the story of the prodigal son begins with the idea of the *identified patient*.[2] Many times in families where there is a great deal of pain the tendency is to focus on one person as the problem. Often the identified patient (or "I.P." in family-therapy shorthand) functions as the lightning rod for the family. The I.P. provides the family with a scapegoat whose problems divert the attention of the family from the problems between the others. The I.P. gives the family a reason for the pain other than the family itself. In the family of the prodigal son, the prodigal is the I.P.

However, God creates families as a whole. Nobody exists on this earth in isolation, as an island. In fact, technically, there are no such things as individuals, only members. We are members of oscillating and changing groups, all pulsing and moving at the same time, all making various demands on us simultaneously. In terms of families, the relationship is the reality. If there is dysfunction, it exists as much *among* people as *within* one person. Therefore, the I.P. can't be *the* problem. The problem belongs to the family as a whole.

In the family described by Jesus in Luke 15, the family's stress and pain manifest themselves in at least two ways: the disengagement of the prodigal; and the enmeshment of the elder son.[3]

The problem of disengagement

"Disengagement" means to unplug, to withdraw, to leave when relationships become stressed. In the extreme it means to sever the relationship as a means of dealing with the strain. It is the dynamic that underlies the action of a teenager who runs away from home or retreats into drugs. To a lesser degree, it is the mind-set of the person who handles family stress by unplugging emotionally, using distance as an emotional buffer, or who becomes a bystander rather than a participant in the family.

In our story, the prodigal son is a severely disengaged person. Note three common characteristics.

"Me First, Me Only"

First of all, he is occupied with a "me-first" and "me-only" attitude. In Luke 15: 12 he demands that he be given his share of the property that supposedly was due him. Very often *the disengaged person becomes preoccupied with the material issues of life rather than the emotional and relation-*

al. "I want what is mine," the person declares. "I don't care if it hurts you. I don't care if it causes you grief. I want what I want."

Uses Physical Distance

Second, *the disengaged person habitually uses physical distance as a means of creating emotional distance.* The son in verse 13 informs the father that he is leaving.

I wonder what went on in that house before he left? Were there fights? What about tears?

I can't imagine the father saying nonchalantly, "Sure, no big deal. Take half of what I own and have a good trip."

The response of the father later in the story indicates the degree of intensity that must have gone on before the son left. The father thought the son had died. The son's leaving was a matter of life and death, not a casual parting.

Problems Always Go with Him

Third, notice what happens to the disengaged person. *No matter how far he goes, he carries the relationship with him.*

In verse 18 he even has a conversation with his father in his head. "I will arise and will go to my father, and I will say . . ."

You can move halfway around the world and still wake up with your mother or father figuratively in your room. Distance rarely solves anything. The knot in the stomach, the tension headache, the conflicts with parentlike people, all are indications of the up-close presence of a parent from whom you are trying to disengage. Disengagement is dysfunctional; it certainly didn't work for the prodigal.

The problem of enmeshment

There is a second person in the story, the elder son. We learn about the elder son only after the prodigal has returned, but we can infer from the dialogue what might have occurred before the wayward one left.

It is likely there was a great deal of strife and tension between the two. It's not inconceivable that the elder son was glad when the prodigal left. He then had the father to himself. Probably he hungered for the father's approval.

The elder son is enmeshed. *"Enmeshment" involves the psychological glue that holds families together. It's a kind of emotional stickiness between us.* In a healthy sense that glue is supposed to loosen and allow us to grow up, leave our families, and start families and/or lives of our own. But in some families that loosening doesn't happen. The people stay stuck together, just like the elder son and the father. Notice some characteristics of the enmeshed person.

Resentment

First of all, *he is plagued by seething resentment.* In verse 28 we read that the elder son "was angry and refused to go in . . ." (RSV). He must have been frustrated. Try as he might he couldn't shake the feelings he had toward his younger brother. On top of all of that, his father was making a big deal over his brother's coming home, and the father had never made a big deal over the elder son. "It's just not fair," he must have thought.

Insecurity

The second characteristic of the enmeshed elder son is that *he is insecure and fearful of being displaced by the prodigal.* "You always did like him more than me," is the underlying theme of the relationship with his father.

Parenthetically, I recall talking with a forty-year-old woman-friend of mine. She was the eldest of four daughters. Their family had just celebrated Christmas, and she had experienced feelings that had been with her for years. When it came time to open presents, she was aware that the youngest daughter, the supposed favored one, had received more presents from the parents than did either of the other three. Forty years old and still worrying about fairness and favoredness! She was chronically insecure and threatened by the younger sister. She was enmeshed and could identify with the elder son.

Triangles

Instead of dealing directly with the father about his feelings toward the father, the elder son uses a third characteristic of the enmeshed person. *He uses triangling as a means of communication.*[4] *"Triangling" refers to a communication pattern in which two people talk to each other about a third person without talking to the third person.* In this case the relationship between the elder son and the prodigal was dealt with through the father. Whenever triangling occurs, the results are inevitably negative. They are by definition dysfunctional.

Suppose, for example, a teenage son is having trouble with his father. They're just not getting along. The son goes to the mother and complains about the father. The mother listens because she is concerned but also because she has some of the same feelings toward the father. The positive emotional valence between the son and the mother never creates a positive emotional valence between the son and the father. In fact, the relationship between the son and the mother is likely to drain off the tension between the other two without requiring them to change. Without meaning to, the mother perpetuates the problem by becoming triangled in.

Although the issue was between the elder son and the father, the focus of the elder son's attention was on the return of the younger. If only he could have said, "Dad, I've enjoyed having this special time with you. Now I'm scared. He's back, and I'm afraid you'll only pay attention to him and not to me. I can't admit to you that I'm insecure and that I'm afraid if you are given the choice you will choose him. I can't tell you how I feel so I'll be mad at him." The triangle is formed out of the elder brother's fear and frustration.

"Poor Me"

The last characteristic of the enmeshed elder son is his "poor me" attitude. *The enmeshed person is forever struggling with feeling like a martyr.* "No one cares," he thinks. "No one recognizes me. No one appreciates the work I do. I always come out on the short end of the stick."

Neither the disengaged nor the enmeshed person ultimately feels good about his family. Only the third kind of person can experience what it means to be free and to be family. The third pattern is the differentiated person.

The pattern of differentiation

In the story of the prodigal son the differentiated person is a compilation of the prodigal who has returned and the father who welcomes him home. *"Differentiated" people are able to distinguish themselves as unique persons, separate from others, and able to determine for themselves the level or degree of emotional closeness between themselves and others.*

Take Responsibility for Themselves

The first characteristic of differentiated people is that *they are able to admit when they're wrong and to forgive when it's needed.* The relationship between the father and the son is marked by the process of reconciliation. Neither demands that the other capitulate. The relationship is able to absorb serious stress and come out at the other end intact.

Free to Come and Go with Ease

A second characteristic is *the ability to establish one's own sense of self to the point he or she can enter and exit the family of origin with comfort.* Differentiated people can come and go from their families without discomfort. They look forward to being with the family and feel good when it's time to leave. Ease and comfort earmark the connecting patterns. It's OK to grow up and leave home. It's OK to like to come home again. It's all right to love others and belong to them, too. The glue between the family members matures to allow comfortable connecting and disconnecting.

Treat Others as Individuals

The third characteristic is modeled by the father. He treats his sons as unique persons and not like a cluster of grapes. Notice that the answer he gives to each son is different and tailored to meet his need. He says to the son who has disengaged, "I'm glad you're back. I thought you were dead. I'm glad you're home." To the elder, enmeshed son he says, "All that I ever had was yours. You were never left out. I care about you as much as I do your brother." To help others differentiate, we must relate to them as individuals rather than as "the kids." In fact, healthy differentiating families are characterized by members who have person-to-person, face-to-face, and one-to-one relationships. Family members aren't offended if they get together individually rather than always as a group. It's all right if someone chooses not to come to a family get-together or a family celebration. They're happy if the person can make it, and they accept it if the person can't. You can be a member of the family and still be an individual within the family.

Refuse to Triangle

The fourth characteristic is also modeled by the father. *He doesn't triangle. He doesn't gossip.* We're not told exactly in the story, but it wouldn't make sense for him to have said to one son about the other, "You'll never guess what your brother said to me about you . . ." He didn't try to work it out between them. Differentiating families let people work things out for themselves.

You'll remember that we were foster parents for two years. Shortly after Jim came, he began to pick on Shannon, our youngest daughter, who was a year younger than he. He would mock her, make fun of her, and make life miserable for her.

Her first response was to dissolve tearfully and come running to Lucy or me for support. Usually I would stomp outside and confront our son with his misdeeds. Jim would coyfully apologize, and a short time later the pattern would repeat itself.

The problem was that Shannon was triangling us in against Jim. Our intervention didn't make things better between the two of them. Instead, we were communicating to Shannon that she was inadequate and that she couldn't function in the world with the people who are older, bigger, and more bullying than she. To Jim we were communicating that he was an outsider and that our loyalties were with Shannon.

Once we recognized the pattern, we both agreed to let Shannon work it out for herself. I can still remember the day. The kids were playing kickball in the street in front of the house. Jim began bullying Shannon as usual. She came running into the house. We refused to intervene, instead encouraging her to work it out for herself.

Her initial response was to feel betrayed, but that passed quickly. With fire in her eyes she turned on her heels and marched outside. Jim could see her coming, and he began to retreat. She put her face directly in front of his and gave him a piece of her mind. Whatever the issue was, she made her point, because he handed her the ball, she walked into the middle of the street, and the game continued.

The special ending to the story is that Shannon eventually bonded to Jim as if he were her own brother. I'm convinced that our strategy that day played a significant role in their relationship. Had we continued in the direction we were heading, they would never have found each other as friends let alone as brother and sister. We stopped our triangling, and they had to work out their relationship for themselves.

Able to Remain Objective

A fifth characteristic mentioned in family-therapy literature is not necessarily found in our story. *Differentiated people are able to remain objective when with their families and that objectivity generalizes to other relationships as well.* To be objective means to not allow the emotional boundaries between people to become so diffuse, or spread so thin, that it's impossible to tell where one person stops and another begins:

An example would be when one family member becomes upset at a situation at school or at work and the other member(s) become equally upset. If someone's mad, we all need to be mad. If one's hurt, we're all hurt. But a healthy sense of objectivity allows each member to decide whether and/or how that individual wishes to respond. The key becomes achieving a balance between objectivity and caring. The differentiated person is able to see others as different from himself or herself and to respond accordingly.

No Flawless Families

God's family is not perfect. He struggles with the problem of prodigals just like we do. He doesn't bat a thousand percent so why should we expect that of ourselves? God has people reject Him continually. So it's not reasonable that we demand of ourselves that our families operate smoothly with no problems or defections. Covenant families are infused with grace and forgiveness, not perfection.

The story of the prodigal son is the story of a covenant family. It is a family marked by repentance when members recognize they are wrong and have injured another. It is a family marked by forgiveness and acceptance of an erring member. And, last of all, it is a growing and changing family.

In spite of the problems of disengagement and enmeshment, they are able to become reconciled to one another. Jesus' clear inference by the end of the story is that when reconciliation is achieved, God's purposes are achieved as well. He would tell us to go and do likewise.

A Brief Summary

Some children go to "a far country" by using patterns of:
*Disengagement—unplugging, withdrawing, leaving when relationships become stressed.
Characteristics:
>—Preoccupied with the material issues of life rather than the emotional and relational.
>—Uses physical distance as a means of creating emotional distance.
>—No matter how far the person goes, he or she carries the relationship right along.

*Enmeshment—the psychological glue that holds families together and sometimes does not loosen to let children make their own lives.
Characteristics:
>—Plagued by resentment.
>—Insecure and fearful of being displaced.
>—Uses triangling as a means of communication. (Two people talk to each other about the third person.)
>—Struggles with feeling like a martyr.

The healthy person uses the pattern of:
*Differentiation—distinguishing oneself as a unique person who is able to determine the level of emotional closeness with others.
Characteristics:
>—Able to admit he or she is wrong and to forgive others.
>—Establishes a sense of self so person can enter and exit the family of origin with comfort.
>—Treats others as individuals.
>—Refuses to triangle.
>—Remains objective.

7

Walls Come Tumbling Down

Recent years have brought a radical shift in how we relate to our environment. Where once developing, logging, and mining interests could pretty well do as they pleased, the process has been altered to the advantage of the environment. Environmental impact studies are now required to shield the land and the wilderness from unrestrained and irresponsible growth.

But who shields families? Who screens laws and regulations for their effect on families? Unfortunately, no one does. We must fend for ourselves. We must sort through the information that bombards us from the media to decide whether or not we will take heed. It is our responsibility to proceed with family impact studies on our own. The task can belong to no one else.

This chapter is written from the perspective of a family impact study. Suggestions are given that are intended to form a kind of topographical map of how family members relate to one another. A topographical map defines the heights, depths, and boundaries of a particular section of land. A family topographical map defines boundaries for family members as they successfully give and take with each other.

Relational Boundaries

My assumption is that the principles generated by the apostle Paul for the church at Ephesus are valid for families in the twentieth century. The relational topography for the church and the family are the same. We both must deal with similar relational boundaries. What is good for the church is good for the family in terms of the quality of relationships that make them up. The church and the family are more alike than unlike when it comes to living and functioning as members together.

Let's discuss three topographical boundaries for the covenant family.

Committed to the resolution of hostility

In Ephesians 2, Paul declares that Christ "is our peace . . . and has broken down the dividing wall of hostility" (v. 14, RSV). The Gospel was envisioned by Paul to have removed the reason for hostility between the Jews and the Greeks, between slaves and slave-owners, and between men and women. The presence of Christ was a unifying force for the apostle. He meant for the church at Ephesus to allow itself to be as influenced by that Presence as he was. In the same way that Jesus calmed the sea, Paul experienced that steadying and calming effect in his life. He placed a high value on peace and unity.

Covenant families are committed to a similar goal. The presence of Christ is a unifying and a calming force. Family members are committed to working things out among themselves and to building their relationships on the foundation of covenant love.

In contrast, much emphasis in our modern world is placed on competing forces. Often that emphasis provokes the opposite effect from that which the Gospel intended for us. Take, for example, what has happened in the behavioral sciences.

Of Fads and Rages

The social and behavioral sciences are as vulnerable to fads as is the clothing design industry. Several years ago we were overrun by the "ventilation of anger" fad.[1] The rule was to let it all hang out. Anger, even hostility, was termed a necessary condition for human intimacy. Counselors like myself spent hours teaching couples and families how to fight. We all bought into the "rage" about rage.

Recently a national study conducted at the University of New Hampshire by the family sociologist Murray Strauss asked whether the ventilation of anger was good for families.[2] Strauss found that venting anger, as it had been propounded during the let-it-all-hang-out era, was destructive and harmful rather than constructive and helpful. Clearly, according to Strauss, the ventilation of anger led to further unrestrained anger and eventually to hostility. The hostility in turn eroded and even sometimes destroyed relationships between the fighting partners. The fad was harmful.

We are told by Paul to live peaceably with one another. We can assume that what was true for the church is true for our families. We are to be committed to peace and to be wary of hostility.[3]

The Litany

Rather than leave us with a lofty goal and no direction for meeting it, in Ephesians 4: 15-32, Paul develops a marvelous litany of relationship designed to help us live in peace with one another. In this passage I have identified a seven-step process; it is Paul's topographical map for handling conflict.[4] The lay of the land includes:

1. Speak the truth in love (v. 15). God intends us to live truthfully with one another. The Gospel that sets us free also enables us to live consistently with that truth.
2. When the truth is spoken it often provokes anger. Handle that anger daily and don't let it build up (v. 26). Satan takes advantage if you let anger build up.
3. When you speak the truth, do so for the purpose of building up or edifying your relationship with the other person rather than tearing it down (v. 29b).
4. When you speak, do so at an appropriate time and place—that is, as fits the occasion (v. 29c).
5. Speak in such a way you can imagine your statements

being used for good in the other's life. "That it may impart grace to those who hear" (v. 29d).

6. Don't let the power of negative emotions control you (v. 31).
7. Rather, be ruled by positive and constructive motives toward the other person (v. 32).

These steps have a hymnlike quality to them. They were meant to lift the spirits of Paul's readers as well as to instruct them. Most of all, they were intended to counter the natural tendency of our human spirit toward hostility and to direct us toward peace and unity.

For covenant families, the implications of Paul's instructions are significant. We are to deal with one another openly and honestly, but within a context of responsibility. The good of the other person is to be a controlling factor, not just our own good. Truth packaged in love and responsibility is the goal we strive for.

Motivated by love and example

Paul's second topographical boundary for covenant families says that Christ has abolished "in his flesh the law of commandments and ordinances" (2: 15, RSV). *Covenant families are to risk motivating by love and example rather than by rules and coercion.*

When you're raising children, sometimes it's easier to believe that you can motivate them by hitting them rather than by loving them. This is particularly true for more authoritarian-type parents. Their fear is that love won't work as a motivating force.

There is a marvelous story in the Old Testament that

illustrates how to motivate people. It is the story of Rehoboam, the son of Solomon (I Ki. 11: 41—12: 20).

At the end of Solomon's 40-year reign over Israel, he became more and more punitive and coercive. When he died, his heir, Rehoboam, wondered whether he should follow in his father's footsteps with the same authoritarian policies or whether he should institute a new day, with policies based on love and covenant.

He went to the older counselors who had known the tyranny of Solomon. "How do you advise me to answer this people?" he asked. Their response indicates the wisdom of age and of those who had survived the old regime: "If you will be a servant to this people today and serve them, and speak good words to them when you answer them, then they will be your servants for ever" (12: 6, 7, RSV). Their counsel was that covenant love motivates unconditionally.

The Thick Finger

But Rehoboam refused the counsel of his elders and instead turned to his contemporaries. "What do you [younger men] advise that we answer this people who have said to me, 'Lighten the yoke that your father put upon us'?" Their answer is the traditional answer of the authoritarian mindset: "Thus shall you say to them, 'My little finger is thicker than my father's loins. And now, whereas my father laid upon you a heavy yoke, I will add to your yoke. My father chastised you with whips, but I will chastise you with scorpions' " (12: 9-11, RSV).

Two drastically different pieces of advice, and Rehoboam implemented the counsel of the younger men rather than the older. He refused to believe that covenant love motivates. He believed more in punishment and coercion.

The result forms one of the saddest narratives in all of Scripture. The people rebelled at his methods and sought to overthrow him as king. He was forced to flee for his life. "So Israel has been in rebellion against the house of David to this day" (12: 19).

Covenant families are those who make the decision to follow God and believe that what motivates them, God's love, will in fact motivate those whom they love. They are those who attempt to follow the wisdom of Rehoboam's elder counselors who say, "Serve and the service itself will provide a way of motivation. Your family will serve you back."

Such decisions require a leap of faith for the parents. They know intimately the folly bound up in the hearts and minds of their children and teenagers. They also know the capriciousness of their own motives and behaviors. But they also know the deep interest God has in their lives and His promise to give them grace and wisdom when they need it most (Heb. 4: 16; Jas. 1: 5).

Covenant families are willing to live with the tension that comes with covenant, and they refuse the supposed safety that comes with contracts and legalism. They are motivated by love and believe love will motivate their loved ones as well.

Committed to reconciliation

The third topographical boundary I would suggest deals with healing. *Covenant family members are restless when they realize something is wrong between them. They have been reconciled to God and believe it is important to be reconciled to one another as well.*

In family therapy literature, the failure to reconcile creates emotional cutoffs.[5] Emotional cutoffs occur when people sever relationships because of unresolved bitterness and hurt. It amazes me that Christians have received reconciliation, the gift of new life in Christ, yet they live with cutoff, broken relationships, many times in their own families.

Jesus said that we are to be reconciled to our brother before we come into the house of God to worship (Mt. 5: 24). We have interpreted this verse to refer to relationships between Christians rather than the relationships in our blood families. I wonder if the thrust of the passage is both/and rather than either/or? Because we culturally allow emotional cutoffs to exist in our families of origin, we easily allow such cutoffs to exist between brothers and sisters in Christ.

For Families, Too

What does the Gospel mean if it doesn't bring wholeness to families? We dilute the efficacy or power of Christ's blood if we think that we can limit reconciliation only to our relationship with Him. Even when we expand our horizons to involve our relationships with other Christians, we diminish the power of the Gospel if we block that power from bringing wholeness to our families.

Jesus has put an end to the reason for hostility between us. Through His death on the cross, He has provided a way for us to be reconciled to one another. There is no excuse for cutoffs other than our own stubbornness and willfulness. Paul said that the hostility had been brought to an end. I'm sure if we could press him on the subject, he would agree that he meant an end to emotional cutoffs between family members as well as within the church body.

But what do you do if you recognize you have emotionally cut off someone in your family? Let me suggest some steps that at least can begin the process of reconciliation.[6]

1. Take responsibility for your own feelings about the person from whom you are alienated. Often we justify the cutoff by assuming we were forced into our decision. That may or may not have been true. But now you have freedom to choose otherwise.

2. Reconstruct the reason(s) why the cutoff took place. Pay attention not only to the facts that brought about the decision but also the feelings that were present at the time. The feeling memories are especially important.
3. Talk about your feelings with someone you trust and with whom you have a relationship of confidentiality. Choose someone who will not sermonize but who will hear you out. Pray with this person about your decision to seek reconciliation. Ask this person to uphold you in prayer as you step out.
4. Develop a plan of action that will put you in personal contact with the one whom you have cut off. Lay plans for face-to-face interaction with the other person. If face-to-face contact is impossible, choose the next best method. A telephone call or calls and letters are an excellent place to begin. In the case of someone who has died, sometimes a letter written to that person as if he or she were still alive is helpful.
5. When the day arrives, speak the truth in love. Own your feelings and the reality of the cutoff. Give the other person space to respond, both literal space (letting the person speak) and emotional space (giving him or her time to experience and express emotions).
6. Take your time and don't plan on quick solutions or easy answers. Be prepared and committed to the long haul rather than the quick fix. The process sometimes takes years.[7]
7. Be prepared to be rebuffed or rejected. Remember, the other person has feelings, too. Your commitment is to do the best you can. You are not responsible for the response(s) of the other person.
8. The process of reconciliation allows the other person the freedom to accept or reject your overtures. We are responsible only for our own choices and not for the choices of others. What is important is that we do our part, not that the other person respond. Sometimes the only benefit that will come out of the process will be the benefit to you personally. You'll know you tried.

Committed to Peace

In Christ God has broken down the greatest of all walls, the wall of alienation and hostility between Himself and the world. In so doing He has given us an example for our relationships with others. Covenant families are committed to living consistently with one another and with the world. The world has yet to see the power of a church that is committed to the whole of the Gospel of reconciliation. Perhaps the place to begin is with families who are committed to that same Gospel.

A Brief Summary

Boundaries for a covenant family include:
   *Willing to resolve hostility.
   *Willing to risk motivating by love and example rather than by rules and coercion.
   *Willing to reconcile their differences.

Strangers and Sojourners No More

"Home," said the poet Robert Frost, "is the place where, when you have to go there, they have to take you in."[1] Definitions abound, but something about his view rings true for me. Home is a place where you belong and where you can be yourself.

Shortly after we were married we moved to Texas to attend seminary. I remember feeling that we were leaving "home." Several times during those early years we "came home" to visit the family either during the summer or at Christmas.

Not until we had children of our own did we begin to feel that home was where we lived. After our first child was born, even though we lived in seminary housing and didn't own a single piece of property anywhere in the world, home was where we lived. It had become a place of safety and identity for me, and I think for all of us. It was our home.

The tragedy of our modern age is that fewer and fewer people have ever experienced a home of their own. The home as a place of safety and identity is becoming an endangered species much like the famed snail darter in the Tennessee rivers.

Paul's letter to the Ephesians establishes clearly that he expected the church to be both a place of safety and a place of identity. Paul indicates that in the Ephesian church all belonged equally. There were to be no distinctions of status, no divisions of privilege, no impenetrable cliques. Jesus Christ had done away with all of that.

For that to be said of any social organization of the first century was remarkable indeed. The world was ruled by Rome and its hierarchy based on power. Greece was viewed as the intellectual center of knowledge and culture. Religious centers abounded as well. In fact, Ephesus was one, the center of the worship of Diana, goddess of the moon. The known world partitioned itself into scores of compartments based on status, wealth, and power.

When Paul wrote his letter to the Ephesian church, he, as much as anyone, was aware of matters of status. Before his conversion, he considered himself religiously superior. He was of an elite class, a Pharisee of the Pharisees (Phil. 3: 4-6). With this in mind, his words recorded in Ephesians 2: 19

90

form a testimony to the remarkable and inclusive grace of God in his life. ". . . No longer strangers and sojourners, but . . . fellow citizens with the saints and members of the household of God" (RSV). The words thunder like the last movement of a Beethoven symphony. They form a crescendo of praise to the God who brought them all together.

If Paul could say this of the Ephesian church, can we not say the same of covenant families? I think so. I would suggest three distinctions of a Christian home, three environmental qualities the covenant family creates for itself and for others.

No one is a stranger

It's hard when you feel like an outsider. It's difficult to be on the outside looking in. It's especially difficult to have belonged somewhere else and to face the loneliness of not belonging where you are now.

We can all remember times when we moved as children or teenagers. The most dreaded adjustment was going to a new school.

The first few days at school were miserable. You walked up the school steps to find your room, and you felt the isolation of being alone. Hundreds of other children may have been there, but it was like you were on an island. Whoever brought you to school left, and you were there all by yourself. The other children walked into the room, and it seemed everyone knew everyone else. Only you were the stranger.

You looked around and noticed how differently you were dressed or how your hair was cut wrong. In general, you felt like you stuck out like a sore thumb.

Quietly you found a seat and hoped no one would come up to claim it. The day was just beginning, but it felt like you had been there for hours. Your first day was the longest day of your life.

As you walked home, you thought to yourself that you would never find a friend. Your memories of friends back where you used to live filled your thoughts, and you were sure nothing would ever be the same. You dreaded the next day.

Day two began like day one. The feelings of loneliness persisted until on the playground another child walked by and said "hello." Shyly you responded only to find out that he or she was new to the school, too. The two of you instantly bonded. You shared a common experience. You were both strangers but no longer alone. Day three didn't seem so ominous.

A stranger is someone who is new among us who doesn't belong. In the first century, to be labeled a Christian was enough to mark you as an outsider. The established social systems considered Christians cultish and bizarre. Wherever Christians went, they didn't belong. Their answer to the problem was to become family to one another. They were like the two new children at school. The presence of another Christian meant you were not alone.

The solution to the isolation and loneliness for the first-century church was the hospitality of the families who made up the church. Such a family was spoken of by the apostle John. It was the household of Gaius, situated probably in Ephesus or at least nearby. Certainly the Ephesian church would have known him and would have appreciated his reputation.

That reputation is recorded for us in John's third letter in the New Testament. The letter is a short testimonial to the hospitality of Gaius and his household. From John we learn of the man's spiritual openness and his generosity toward others. From Gaius we learn what it means as covenant families to minister to others.

We Should . . .

First of all, John commends Gaius for the truth of his life (v. 3). Evidently he had achieved a life-style that was congruent

92

with what he believed; Gaius was not a hypocrite. He had made it a habit to follow the truth.

Second, he had rendered service to the brethren (v. 5). Gaius willingly shared his home and his resources with those who were fellow Christians, especially those who were known to him. He was probably a wealthy man, and therefore the church leaned on him and his resources more than was typical.

Third, and much to his credit, he rendered service to strangers (v. 5). It's one thing to be open and friendly to those you know; it's quite another to relate to those you don't. "Strangers" in this context probably refers to itinerant evangelists who were on the road preaching the Gospel. They would have come with their foreign ways and customs. Their looks, their talk, even their smell would have been different. Had there not been a Gaius and his household, they would have been lonely and resourceless. But the grace of God working in Gaius's life and in the lives of those who lived with him allowed him to accept and to include those aliens into the safety of his home.

Fourth, and last of all, Gaius loved the church (v. 6). He couldn't do or give enough. Jesus Christ had touched his life and that touch demanded that he relate to Christ's new Body with love and concern. The church of the first century was built on the hospitality and love of men and women like Gaius. They formed the basis upon which the church was founded just as much as the apostles, the evangelists, and the prophets did. We, today, are heirs of that tradition.

We Should Not . . .

But the church wasn't made up only of Gaius-like people. John in the same letter tells us of one who lived in marked contrast to Gaius. He tells us of Diotrephes (v. 9). Diotrephes is the downside of the hospitality equation. He models what we are not to be. Note, briefly, the characteristics John attributes to him.

He was selfish; he challenged John's authority as an apostle; he was contentious; and he encouraged exclusivity in the church rather than inclusivity. Had it been left up to Diotrephes, the Body of Christ would have died a sterile death within a few years.

It's difficult to believe that one can have the spirit of Diotrephes and still prosper in the faith. The qualities he demonstrated are antithetical to what it means to live as a covenant people. Still, we all are tempted to manifest his temperament at times. Selfishness, rebelliousness, contentiousness, and exclusivity are very real temptations for the church in today's world. But they are not God's way.

The model for the covenant family is Gaius. He was conscientious and open in his faith. He was generous and loving toward the church. And most of all, he was hospitable to the brethren and to strangers. Had you or I visited him, we would have felt right at home.

All We, Like Strangers

Ours is a world full of strangers, with alienation the watchword of the last half of the twentieth century. We have lost the ability to reach out and connect with one another. There is an existential ache in the soul of modern man that comes from not belonging. The ache is real, and the answer to that ache, ultimately, is Jesus Christ. Although the one who feels estranged bears some responsibility for taking initiative, the initiative in the main falls on the shoulders of others. Who might those others be?

I think that both now and in the future one of the most effective witnesses for Christ is a home in which people love one another and whose members are genuinely hospitable. The day is now here when covenant families must carry the weight of ministry as did Gaius in his day. The church is a place where no one should ever feel like a stranger. To paraphrase Robert Frost, the home of the covenant family is a place where, when you go there, they take you in and you feel like you belong.

No one is a sojourner

The word "stranger" involves the idea of not belonging. Similarly, behind the word "sojourner" is the idea of impermanence. The Christian world of the first century struggled with the problem of transience. They were migrants moving from place to place according to the whim of the local governor or the pressure of persecution. Theirs was a world of temporary quarters and forced journeys. They would have empathized with our transient and throwaway society.

As a means of responding to this pressure, Paul encouraged the church to be a place where Christians could slow their journey and put down roots. They were no longer sojourners. Their world view could take on a different hue because it wasn't colored by the fading tones of temporary relationships. They could believe in one another and trust one another to be there tomorrow. The tyranny of uncertainty could be dealt with in the certainty of their commitment to one another.

Such is the witness of the covenant family. We live in a world shrink-wrapped in plastic and ready to be used once and thrown away. In contrast, the home of the covenant family is a place where a sense of permanence is established. The value of something that lasts is authenticated here. People are more important than things, and their eternal value determines the significance of how they are treated. You don't throw away people; you throw away things. The two are not to be confused, even though the world seems to have reversed the order.

Imagine the influence of the church were we to model for the world the idea of permanence. Rather than tossing the broken pieces of relationships out and starting with new ones, the church would demonstrate that those relationships can be mended and made as good as new. Security builds upon the foundation of certainty, and certainty demands the quality of permanence. Those who are sojourners expect to move on. Those who are no longer sojourners can expect to stay put. The challenge for the covenant family is to learn how to model what the church is to be: a place where people can stay put.

All feel connected

Strangers and sojourners are vulnerable to feeling disconnected. Where and to whom do they belong? The answer to this forms a major theme in the drama of the first-century church as well as the drama of modern society.

Connected to the Past

In terms of the first century, Paul instructed the Ephesians that they came from strong and deep roots. In Christ they were "built upon the foundation of the apostles and prophets . . ." (2: 20, RSV). The church at Ephesus was reminded by Paul that theirs was not a religious movement based on a passing fad. They had every right to feel related to a deep and continuing religious history. The church could have a sense of corporate history.

In terms of modern society, the covenant family seeks to provide its members with similar instruction. It values its religious heritage and its own personal history. Like the apostle Paul the covenant family establishes for its members a sense of feeling connected to the past. It's important that we not feel brand new in the sense of being the first generation of people who are following Christ. History and tradition are valued commodities. Why? Because to have a sense of the past accomplishes at least three things.

In the first place, feeling connected to the past relieves anxiety about both the present and the future based on the experience of our corporate and personal history. As human persons we tend to forget, at least in our current generation, that there is, indeed, nothing new under the sun. What has gone on before is prototype for what is happening today. Thus, we can plan for tomorrow by understanding both yesterday and today. History has a past, present, and future tense. Neither today nor tomorrow will unfold in a vacuum.

Consequently, covenant families frequently rehearse their redemption history. Children of all ages love to hear about the good old days. In the light of the need for a connection to the past, parents are free to speak of their own conversions or their own early religious experiences. They talk comfortably of how God has been at work in their lives in the past, and thus they expect Him to provide in the future.

It's even good to frequently rehearse the personal religious and spiritual history of the children, lest they forget and think they have to start all over. In contrast with modern society, covenant families, like the church at Ephesus, know what foundation they are built upon. They feel connected to the past and are able to use that connectedness to face their anxieties about the future.

In the second place, feeling connected to the past provides a pattern for behavior and expectations. "How should we act? What did you do when . . .? Is it fair for me to expect . . .?" The answers to these open-ended questions are key in terms of providing guidelines for our conduct. Shorn of the past, guidelines are up for grabs. But linked to the past, guidelines have a context and a rationale. The past thus provides a kind of behavioral boundary for the future experience of the younger generation.

Last of all, feeling connected to the past provides for transmission of valuable cultural traditions from one generation to the next. In the Old Testament, Israel built altars and monuments to stand as witnesses to future generations of the

grace and lovingkindness of God (cf. Deut. 6: 10-25). Covenant families create the same kind of traditions as a means of
celebrating the love of God.

In our home, perhaps the most treasured tradition we
have centers around Christmas Eve. Years ago Lucy decided
that on the night before Christmas we would have a picnic in
front of the Christmas tree. She made up special and tasty
foods, each designed to bring an exclamation of joy from the
family. After our supper picnic, we then celebrated com-
munion. Since that time we have followed the same tradition
as all of us celebrate our relationship with God together. Our
extended family has joined us, and it has become for all of us
one of the most treasured spiritual experiences of the year.
Through that tradition we pass on to our children what is
truly important to us. We feel connected to something
meaningful to our past through the use of traditions.

Connected to the Present

But it's also important to feel connected to the present,
which is accomplished by maintaining a sense of interdependence upon one another. We are one another's present tense. We establish for each other how we will experience the present. In so doing, we are writing today in our
memories how we will remember the present tomorrow.

If I could only remember this, it would remind me to be
careful how I relate to those closest to me. We are building
memories, memories of the relationships we share. A harsh
word, an intemperate comment, a misfounded criticism, all
are filed into the memories of their recipients. Likewise a
kind word, a moment of praise, and the reward of recognition
are the building blocks from which memories of today are
constructed.

When I think of feeling connected to the present, I think of
another dimension as well, linkages and networks. In terms
of information theory, the ways in which social systems are
linked to one another determine the effectiveness of their
interdependence. If they are poorly linked, the systems will

feel isolated and will likely operate inefficiently. If they are comfortably and competently linked, they will maximize their effectiveness through their shared experiences and support.

For example, suppose family members are in the habit of criticizing one another and relating to one another judgmentally. If something goes wrong, blame must be affixed. But what happens when a family member needs the support of the others because of a mistake or a problem? The criticism and the judgment of the present tense determines the pattern of the future. That family member will hesitate and/or resist bringing the problem to the family lest judgment fall. When the person needs it most, the family is not there because the right to be there was forfeited in previous interactions.

Connected to the Future

Paul said of the Ephesian church that its members were a "holy temple in the Lord" and "a dwelling place of God in the Spirit" (2: 21, 22, RSV). Although these words have a present-tense dimension to them, I would like to focus on their future dimension as they relate to a covenant family.

Covenant families, like the church, are participating in the future as they accomplish their purposes in the present. The kingdom of God isn't just some time in the vague and distant future (Mt. 6:10; 25: 34). The kingdom of God is also now (Rom. 14: 17; Col. 1: 13). What God intends the world to become determines what we make of the world today. We know from Scripture that He will cause the lion to lie down with the lamb and that there will be war no more. It will be good.

A covenant family is good, too. Because its members are a holy temple in the Lord and a dwelling place for God in the here and now, they form a microcosm of Christ's reign. They work at living peaceably with one another and strive to put their fightings aside. Even if they cannot bring about peace between nations and cannot stop the craziness of the modern arms race, they can change the way they live together and influence others. It is natural that they feel they cannot control the macroevents of the superpowers. They can control, however, their immediate environment and the relationships that make it up. Who knows which is the metaphor for the other, the lion and the lamb lying down together or family members living in peace with one another. Both, it seems, are a miracle of God.

A Brief Summary

Three distinctions in the environment of the covenant family creates:
  *No one is a stranger (someone who doesn't belong).
  *No one is a sojourner (someone who is transient).
  *All feel connected—to the past (through religious heritage and personal history).
                            —to the present (writing memories for each other).
                            —to the future (working at living peacefully together in preparation for Christ's reign).

Transitional People

We have now come full circle—to the issues that were reflected in chapter one. How does a person change attitudes and behaviors if need to change is recognized? Think of the beleaguered mother of chapter one with rebellious children, absent husband, and a tendency to motivate her family through guilt. Having read the book thus far, she would have grown increasingly impatient. Her impatience would be understandable. Her demands are fair. We cannot write and speak of ideals without providing practical solutions. The Philippian jailer asked the question, "What must I do to be saved?" Our mother would ask, "What can I do to change?"

Change isn't easy

Digging In

A transition is defined as passing from one condition to another. In grammar the effective use of transitions aids the reader and helps him or her follow the writer's ideas and/or logic. In life, transitional people stand, as it were, on a bridge between two markedly different patterns of behavior or systems of relationships.[1]

Transitional people decide that the dysfunction of the past, especially that which is transmitted through the generations, stops with them. They dig their heels in and refuse to pass the craziness on to their children. Most often they have grown weary of the struggle and pain of their lives and have decided not to inflict that pain on those they love.

It's easy to say that you'll be a transitional person; it's another thing to actually bring about the change.

102

Our Heritage

The issues we have discussed in this book have taproots deep in the soil of our generational past. Rarely are we talking about something that begins with us; we can see the patterns of our problems in the people who make up our family tree. The research to discover those patterns is called a *genogram*,[2] which is a graphic representation of the people who make up a family of origin, along with a description of their emotional and relational patterns. A genogram will usually pick up the dysfunctional patterns that get in the way of our ability to function well within our own family.

Whether the dysfunctional pattern is chronic alcoholism, psychosomatic illness (illness that has its causes in the mind rather than in the body), or the tendency to deal with relational stress using "cutoffs," or any of a score of other patterns, the patterns have their genesis in deeply held emotional and intellectual generational grooves. Once a trail has been forged, it's much easier to travel down the same trail and its well-worn ruts. The same holds true with the tendency to recreate past problems in the context of the present. It's easy to decide that you'll be a transitional person. It's another to make yourself steer clear of the emotional ruttedness of the people who make up your past.

Momentum also creates an environment in which it's difficult to change. Suppose you were the engineer of a long freight train traveling along a roadbed at 60 miles per hour. You see something that warns you of danger ahead. You slam on the brakes, but because of the weight of the cars behind you, it's several hundred yards—even a mile—before you can stop the train. The force that carries you forward is momentum.

The same momentum occurs in emotional and relational difficulties that are rooted in the past. The generations create a kind of dysfunctional weight that works against the will and energy of the transitional person. You can decide that you are going to do things differently, but when you try, there's a whole lot more work to it than one would imagine.

The third reason change usually is difficult for the transitional person is that change in us demands change in others. The issue is more than an individual psychological matter; it is systemic. By "systemic" I mean that the emotional networks of which we are a part, especially our family, must change when we do or two things tend to happen. The change will force the dysfunction to appear elsewhere as a problem suffered by someone else, or the system itself will dissolve because of the change.[3] This kind of change is hard on people even though on the surface it would appear the change is for the best.

Because of the ruttedness, momentum and systemic change, the transitional person needs to remember that change doesn't come easily.

God Will Help

Change is a necessary dimension of the Christian life. According to Paul, "We all . . . are being changed into his likeness . . ." (II Cor. 3: 18, RSV). Even though we may be "born again," the process has only begun. God Himself continues His investment in us as He makes us into the kind of people He wants us to be. We are to come to Him when we are in need, and He can help (Heb. 4: 16). It is the nature of God to provide mercy and grace at those times.

In Christ we are "a new creation; the old has passed away, behold, the new has come" (II Cor. 5: 17). There is a constant "becoming" quality to the Christian life. We are unfolding daily as testimonies of God's grace and love. There is no reason to believe that God's grace can't touch the generational and relational areas of our lives in the same way it touches the spiritual and the moral. In some ways the "old" of the generational past is more determinative of our present-day attitudes and behaviors than is the "old" of personal and moral choices. The idea is to open both up to the power of God and believe He is willing and able to provide the mercy and grace we need to change.

104

Understanding the issues

Patterns from the Past

In chapter three we discussed five kinds of children who might find it difficult to accept the grace of God because of how they were parented. These patterns of misparenting often lay beneath the surface of our consciousness and intrude into the way we function in our adult lives. Much like a bruise that has been calloused over, these patterns inflicted hurt and pain that never healed. The emotional calluses form to cover the hurt and to keep it from dominating the person's ability to function. Inevitably, as adults, the hurts get in our way.

It's important to realize that the feeling memories of the earlier pain do not necessarily go away simply with the passage of time or because they are no longer consciously on the surface. Such is the deceptiveness of the callus. Because you no longer feel the pain, the tendency is to believe that the hurt has healed. When those hurts infringe into the present, they often do so under the guise of defensive reactions, or the tendency to overcompensate for past deprivations.

Not only do past patterns show up as emotional calluses, but they also show up in role confusion. The inadequate models we experienced in our growing-up years come back to haunt us in feelings of inadequacy about the roles we must perform in the here and now.

It's difficult to be a good husband if you have never seen one in operation. It's hard to function as an affectionate spouse or parent if your earlier role models were never affectionate. The behaviors that are needed, such as giving affection, seem cumbersome or uncomfortable. It's as if we were being asked to build a second house with blueprints that produced a deficient or defective first house. Many of us suffer from this feeling of discomfort in role confusion but have never attributed the discomfort to the inadequacy of our earlier role models.

Expectations in the Present

It seems to me that these patterns from the past have at least two possible major effects on us in the present.

In the first place, they can provoke a fear of relationships. For example, some people never marry because they are afraid to. They carry around the memories of abuse and/or conflict they saw lived out in their parents' marriage. "If that's what marriage is all about, I want nothing to do with it," they say to themselves. Others may carry the fear of being a parent inside them because of their experiences of being misparented.

All in all, the overwhelming sensation is one of fear. The obvious solution is never to marry or never to have children. Whatever the decision, the motivation beneath it is the anxiety that the past will repeat itself in the present.

The second way the patterns from the past can affect us is in the area of expectations.[4] When we marry, all of us come into that relationship with presumptions of what the nature of marriage will or should be and the kind of relationship we will have with our spouse. Part of our attraction to the person we marry has to do with these expectations.[5]

If we experienced misparenting in our earlier parent/child relationship, the tendency is to expect the spouse to make up or compensate us for that experience. For example, the abused child-become-adult might expect the spouse never to be abusive, even to the point of never raising his or her voice. The neglected child-become-adult expects the spouse to constantly nurture or be tolerant of the spouse's hyperindependence. The pampered child-become-adult expects to be spoiled, and so forth for each parenting style.

106

I am convinced that many of the abiding frustrations experienced by people in their marriages stem from this phenomenon. We expect our spouses to care for us in ways we were not cared for by our parents, to perform in ways our parents failed to perform. The problem with these expectations is that our spouses inevitably fail to meet them. They fail because we are asking them to be parent and spouse simultaneously. It's impossible to be someone's husband and to be her father, too, to be someone's wife and to be his mother. The roles are conflicting.

As a result, more often than not, the marriage collapses under the weight of the conflicting demands and the frustrations of unmet expectations. Two people end up habitually unhappy with one another yet not really knowing why. A marriage is not meant to bear that kind of weight, and it fails or, at the least, is constantly stressed.

Repetition of the Pattern

What happens when a person's spouse fails to "parent" him or her? The dysfunction passes to the relationship with the next generation. That the pattern repeats itself in the next parent/child relationship makes sense. The parent/child relationship forms one axis and the spousal relationship another. The one who is child in the first parent/child relationship has become the parent in the second. The dysfunction flows naturally along channels that move in the same direction. The spousal channel, if we can call it that, flows in a different direction.

When the spousal relationship falters, the pressure transfers to the new parent/child relationship. Consequently, the tendency is for the new parent to operate at one of two extremes: to parent using the same dysfunctional patterns as that person experienced as a child or to react to that pattern and to overcompensate in the other direction. Either alternative results in passing the pattern from one generation to the next. Unfortunately, the problems tend to get worse as they pass from parent to child to parent to child.[6]

What can be done?

The place to begin the task of transition is to take inventory of oneself. Answer the following questions:

1. If you had to choose, which one or two of the parenting styles discussed in chapters three and four would best represent your mother and father's parenting style? How were your parents different from one another? How were they the same? How is your parenting style like theirs? How are you different?

2. Can you remember any times as a child that were especially painful? Who were the people involved? What is your relationship with them now? Are you cut off from anyone, or have you cut anyone off? What would it take to heal those relationships?

3. As best as you can remember, what are your memories of your parents' marital relationship? Again, how is your marriage like theirs? How is it different?

4. What can you identify in terms of generational patterns that might explain what is happening in your significant relationships today? What about the significant relationships of family members? Take the time to do a genogram if you need more specific information.

5. Ask your family to answer questions 1-4 about you. Be prepared to hear some answers you like and some that you don't. Work at not being defensive. Use the discussion as an opportunity to open up communication between you.

6. What expectations might you have regarding your spouse that stem from your unmet needs as a child? Talk it over with your family. What needs might they have? Where did their needs come from? Again, use it as an opportunity to grow.

Be prepared for the process to take time. Sometimes matters such as these move with glacial speed, and the tendency is to become impatient.

Support One Another

The grace of God most often comes wrapped in the form of support from another believer. To face these issues, we really do need one another. I would suggest:

1. Find an individual or a group who will listen to you and work with you on the issues as you discover them. Although it's good to share these matters with your spouse, it's better if you discuss them with not only your spouse but also someone else. Perhaps it would be good to start a group to explore these issues together.
2. Pray for one another. Be prepared to list items specifically to be brought before the Lord. Don't underestimate the power and concern of God in the process.
3. If you or someone in your group discovers issues that are difficult to handle, be prepared to seek out professional counseling. Sometimes it's better to face these issues with someone who is experienced at handling painful matters. Don't be ashamed if you need help. We all do at one time or another.

A Brief Summary

Even when one decides to be a transitional person, committed to ending dysfunctional patterns, change is not easy. Past parenting patterns tend to be repeated and to become more emphatic. But by examining those patterns, enlisting the support of others, and asking God for grace and mercy, the patterns can be broken.

Future possibilities

If you and I are to be transitional people, we will need all the help we can get. I am of the opinion that it is time for the Church, the Body of Christ, to lead us into a discussion of these issues. The marvelous thought is that, if we are able to "work out our own salvation" in this way, we will change the patterns of relationships for generations to come. What is at stake is not only our peace and joy but also that of our children and our grandchildren. It's true that the sins of the fathers can pass "upon the children to the third and the fourth generation" (Ex. 20: 5, RSV). It is also true that the blessings of God can pass to the same three or four generations if we are able to change the patterns. The future for those we love begins with us.

Endnotes

Chapter One

1. A similar multiple-level analysis is suggested in the works of Ivan Boszormenyi-Nagy, *Invisible Loyalties* (New York: Harper and Row, 1973); and "Contextual Family Therapy," in the *Handbook of Family Therapy*, Alan S. Gurman and David P. Kniskern, eds. (New York: Brunner/Mazel, 1981).
2. See Helm Stierlin, *Psychoanalysis and Family Therapy* (New York: Jason Aronson, 1977).
3. For examples of the nature of systems as they apply to families, see Salvador Minuchin, *Families and Family Therapy* (Cambridge: Harvard University Press, 1974); and J. Haley, *Problem-solving Therapy* (San Francisco: Jossey-Bass, 1976).
4. Perhaps the most significant discussion of the issue of communication in families has taken place in the works of Don Jackson and Paul Watzlawick. See Don Jackson, *Human Communication*, Vols. 1 and 2 (Palo Alto: Science and Behavior Books, 1968); and Paul Watzlawick, *Pragmatics of Human Communication* (New York: Basic Books, 1967) and *The Language of Change* (New York: Basic Books, 1977).
5. For the classic discussion of the theory of the "double bind," see Gregory Bateson, Don Jackson, John Weakland, and Jay Haley, "Toward a theory of schizophrenia," *Behavioral Science*, 1956, 1, pp. 251-264.

6. The nature of metacommunication is discussed at length by Paul Watzlawick, *Pragmatics of Human Communication* (New York: Basic Books, 1967).

Chapter Two

1. This is the definition suggested by James Torrance, "Reformed Theology: A critique of the Covenant concept," transcript of a colloquium presented at Westmont College, April, 1975.
2. I am indebted to Ray S. Anderson of Fuller Theological Seminary for his discussion of this idea.
3. See James Torrance, ibid.
4. See James Torrance, ibid.
5. Such is the distinction made by Donald Tweedie in his thoughts about "Covenant Therapy," unpublished manuscript, nd.

Chapter Three

1. See Lawrence Richards, *A Theology of Christian Education* (Grand Rapids: Zondervan, 1975).
2. See Audrey M. Berger, "The child abusing family," *American Journal of Family Therapy*, 1980, Vol. 8, No. 4, pp. 52-68.
3. See the *Los Angeles Times*, May 19, 1983.
4. The term "neglect" is used here as it is defined by Dorothy Baumrind, "Current patterns of parental authority," *Developmental Psychology Monographs*, 1971, Vol. 4, pp. 1-103.
5. The child-centered marriage is discussed by Virginia Satir, *Peoplemaking* (Palo Alto: Science and Behavior Books, 1972).
6. See Ivan Boszormenyi-Nagy, *Invisible Loyalties* (New York: Harper and Row, 1973).
7. See the discussion on the parental child, Virginia Satir, *Conjoint Family Therapy* (Palo Alto: Science and Behavior Books, 1967).

Chapter Four

1. This idea is suggested in the excellent chapter by Kenneth Terkelsen, "Toward a theory of the life cycle," in *The Family Life Cycle: A Framework for Family Therapy*, E. Carter and M. McGoldrick, eds. (New York: Gardner Press, 1980).
2. The distinction between "what" and "how" is suggested by Paul Watzlawick in *Pragmatics of Human Communication* (New York: Basic Books, 1967).
3. See Erik Erikson, *Childhood and Society* (New York: Norton, 1950); and "Identity and the life cycle," *Psychological Issues*, 1(1), pp. 18-171, 1959.

Chapter Five

1. See Gerhard Kittel, "Akouo," *Theological Dictionary of the New Testament*, Vol. 1 (Grand Rapids, Mich.: Wm. B. Eerdman's Publishing Co., 1964), pp. 223-224.

Chapter Six

1. That several churches provide such support yet are unaware of one another is mute commentary on the need for a network of such groups.
2. See Salvador Minuchin, *Families and Family Therapy* (Cambridge: Harvard University Press, 1974).
3. See Murray Bowen, *Family Therapy in Clinical Practice* (New York: Jason Aronson, 1978).
4. See S. Minuchin, B. Rosman, and L. Baker, *Psychosomatic Families* (Cambridge: Harvard University Press, 1978).

Chapter Seven

1. See George Bach, *The Intimate Enemy* (New York: William Morrow and Co., 1969).

2. See Murray Strauss, "Leveling, civility and violence in the family," *Journal of Marriage and the Family*, Vol. 36, February, pp. 13-30.

3. See Richard Gelles, *The Violent Home* (Beverly Hills: Sage Publications, 1974).

4. I have discussed the issue of the resolution of anger in *If I'm So Free, How Come I Feel Boxed In?* (Waco, Tex.: Word Books, 1978).

5. The nature of emotional cutoffs is discussed by Eileen Pendagast, "A guide to the genogram," *The Family*, Vol. 5, No. 1.

6. For a practical yet thoroughly professional article about reconciliation from a secular perspective, see James Framo, "The family of origin as a therapeutic resource . . . You can and should go home again," *Family Process*, 1976, 15, pp. 193-210.

7. The long-term character of the differentiation process is discussed by Murray Bowen, *Family Therapy in Clinical Practice* (New York: Jason Aronson, 1978).

Chapter Eight

1. "Death of a Hired Man," *Complete Poems of Robert Frost* (Henry Holt and Company, Inc., 1930).

Chapter Nine

1. I am indebted to my good friend Carlfred Broderick from the University of Southern California for introducing me to this concept.

2. See Eileen Pendagast, "A guide to the genogram," *The Family*, Vol. 5, No. 1.

3. See Salvador Minuchin, *Families and Family Therapy* (Cambridge: Harvard University Press, 1974).

4. See Clifford Sager, *Marriage Contracts and Couple Therapy* (New York: Brunner/Mazel, 1976).

5. See Helm Stierlin, *Psychoanalysis and Family Therapy* (New York: Jason Aronson, 1977).

6. See W. Robert Beavers, "A Theoretical Basis for Family Evaluation," *No Single Thread: Psychological Health in Family Systems*, Jerry M. Lewis, et. al. (New York: Brunner-Mazel, 1976).